P9-AGS-053

"During my pregnancy, I had days of quiet contentment, and days in which I felt joyously connected. . . . I also had days of intense anxiety about my baby-to-be's health, about labor, about my weight gain. . . . I was alternately excited and nervous, plus eager to prepare myself as much as possible. The book I craved to have as a confidence guide during my pregnancy is this book—in fact, much of it was researched and written while I was pregnant. . . ."

—JANIS GRAHAM
from the Introduction

❧ ❧ ❧

Month-by month, step-by-step, *Your Pregnancy Companion* will help you cope with the myriad decisions and concerns of pregnancy, including:

- Fears caused by a previous miscarriage (Remember: after a single miscarriage, your odds of having a normal pregnancy are the same as for a woman who never miscarried)
- Whether to have amniocentesis and other prenatal tests
- Toxins to avoid at home and at work
- Sharing your news/starting to "show"—reactions from strangers, co-workers, and friends
- Symptoms of preterm labor, and medical tactics to delay delivery
- Circumcision pros and cons
- Preparing your firstborn for the arrival of a sibling

Easy to read, accurate and steadfastly realistic, *Your Pregnancy Companion* gives you the knowledge you need for a pregnancy with a minimum of stress, and a maximum of joy!

YOUR
Pregnancy
COMPANION

A Month-by-Month Guide
to All You Need to Know
Before, During and After Pregnancy

J A N I S   G R A H A M

with a foreword by
Miriam Greene, M.D.

POCKET BOOKS
New York   London   Toronto   Sydney   Tokyo   Singapore

To Bob, of course

The author of this book is not a physician, and the ideas, procedures, and suggestions in this book are not intended as a substitute for the medical advice of a trained health professional. All matters regarding your health require medical supervision. Consult your physician before adopting the suggestions in this book, as well as about any condition that may require diagnosis or medical attention. The author and publishers disclaim any liability arising directly or indirectly from the use of this book.

Illustrations by Jose Diaz

The tables on pages 91–93 were reprinted from *Jane Brody's Nutrition Book* by Jane Brody, by permission of W. W. Norton & Company, Inc., copyright © 1981 by Jane E. Brody.

The chart on page 54 was reprinted from *Nutrition for Your Pregnancy* by Judith E. Brown, by permission of University of Minnesota Press, copyright © 1983 by The University of Minnesota.

An *Original* Publication of POCKET BOOKS

POCKET BOOKS, a division of Simon & Schuster Inc.
1230 Avenue of the Americas, New York, NY 10020

Copyright © 1991 by Janis Graham

All rights reserved, including the right to reproduce
this book or portions thereof in any form whatsoever.
For information address Pocket Books, 1230 Avenue
of the Americas, New York, NY 10020

Graham, Janis.
    Your pregnancy companion : a month-by-month guide to all you need
to know before, during, and after pregnancy / Janis Graham ; with a
foreword by Miriam Greene ; [illustrations by Jose Diaz].
        p.   cm.
    Includes index.
    ISBN 0-671-68557-0 : $8.95
    1. Pregnancy—Popular works.   I. Title.
RG525.G65   1991
618.2'4—dc20

91-3958
CIP

First Pocket Books trade paperback printing August 1991

10   9   8   7   6   5   4   3   2   1

POCKET and colophon are registered trademarks of
Simon & Schuster Inc.

Cover illustration by Lisa Adams
Cover design by Cathy Sahsa
Text design by Stanley S. Drate/Folio Graphics Co. Inc.

Printed in the U.S.A.

CONTENTS

ぶ 3

ぶ 4

❧ 5

❧ 6

7

8

৯ 9

৯ 10

❧ 11

FOREWORD

As an obstetrician and mother of two, I've experienced pregnancy from many angles. And I've come to believe that there are two things that an expectant mother needs in order for her pregnancy to be an unforgettable and fulfilling adventure.

First, I feel it is of utmost importance that a woman have a give-and-take relationship with her doctor. While technological advances and knowledge of maternal/fetal medicine have made pregnancy and childbirth easier and safer, these technologies and interventions involve choices that can be intimidating. And so a woman needs to feel that she and her doctor are part of a team—a team in which she plays an active role in the decision-making process. Only then can she and her doctor work together effectively to do what's best for her and her baby.

I also know that we are all apprehensive of what is unknown to us. So for confidence and self-assurance, every expectant mother needs to have a firm understanding of all the different bodily changes, medical treatments, and checkup tests that may be encountered during a pregnancy. And that's precisely where this book comes in: in the pages that follow the reader will become familiar with virtually every important facet of pregnancy.

There are many wonderful aspects to this book, the first being the simple style it is written in. Everything is explained in such clear and concise language that it is easy to understand the physiology of pregnancy and the technical procedures that are performed during pregnancy and labor.

The fact that the book is organized as a month-by-month "calendar" gives the expectant mother a convenient reference guide to those changes taking place within her body at a specific time during the pregnancy. So a woman may peer toward the future and see what is in store for her in the months ahead. Diets, exercise programs, and procedures are also addressed sensibly in separate sections, with diagrams and easy-to-follow instructions. The book is comprehensive, too: it not only addresses the woman who is interested in becoming pregnant, but it provides a resource guide to breast-feeding and support groups that might be helpful after pregnancy.

But most important in my opinion is that Janis Graham brings a personal touch to the book, depicting the emotional ups and downs that take place during these sometimes anxious nine months. There are mood swings that are hormonally controlled, and there are aspects of labor and delivery that every woman anticipates or fears, and the author helps every woman navigate these feelings and experiences successfully.

As pregnancy nears its end, a new phase of life begins for a woman. Motherhood brings with it a whole new set of challenges and responsibilities. A woman becomes part of the exclusive club of motherhood, and reading *Your Pregnancy Companion* is an initiation into this club. It is written by a mother with the warmth and sincerity that we all expect to have when we become parents.

Enjoy this book, and most of all enjoy your pregnancy. It is a most exciting time in your life.

MIRIAM GREENE, M.D.
Clinical Instructor of Obstetrics and Gynecology
New York University Medical School

INTRODUCTION

During my pregnancy, I wasn't obsessive in my worrying, but I wasn't carefree, with faith that I would instinctively know what to do, either. I had days of quiet contentment, days in which I hardly thought about being pregnant, and days punctuated with a sort of spiritual expansiveness in which I felt joyously connected to all the women who had given birth before me and to all those who would give birth after me. I also had days of intense fearfulness about my baby-to-be's health, days of anxiety about labor and labor pains, days of freaking out over my weight gain, days of being plagued with ambivalent feelings about having a baby. Overall, I suppose I felt the way I do whenever I face something new: I was alternately excited and nervous, plus eager to cultivate my confidence by preparing myself as much as possible.

The book I craved to have as a confidence guide during my pregnancy is this book—in fact, much of it was researched and written while I was pregnant (I completed the manuscript on my daughter's first birthday). I've tried to avoid exaggerated warnings, impossible-to-implement prescriptions, and glossed-over reassurances (the things I found so annoying in other pregnancy books). Instead, I've simply tried to tell the "straight" story on pregnancy. By that, I mean, I've aimed to produce a resource that is not only accurate, up-to-date, and comprehensive, but is, above all, steadfastly realistic in its advice.

There are many people who deserve thanks for the help they've given me in making this book become a reality:

• Susan Millar Perry, formerly an editor at *Self* magazine, who had faith in me as a young, just-getting-started writer and who gave me my first big assignment on the subject of pregnancy

• Lois de la Haba, my former literary agent, for encouraging me to pursue my interest in writing a book on pregnancy

• Sally Peters, my editor at Pocket Books, for her initial interest and committed enthusiasm

• Miriam Greene, M.D., for her invaluable feedback and criticisms

• the American College of Obstetricians and Gynecologists, the International Childbirth Education Association, La Leche League, Health Education Associates, and the American College of Nurse-Midwives for the slew of excellent information they print on pregnancy

• Robert Kuehn, my husband, for his enduring confidence in me

• Cindy Graham, my sister, for the wisdom and support she was so generous with during my pregnancy, as well as for her criticisms of this book

• Charles Debrovner, M.D., Alison Ho, M.D., and Judith de Celis, M.D., my obstetricians/gynecologists, for the excellent care they gave me before, during, and after my pregnancy

• Friends who were pregnant as I wrote this book, for taking the time to read the manuscript and giving me their honest reactions

JANIS GRAHAM

1

PREPARING FOR PREGNANCY: READ THIS IF YOU'RE NOT PREGNANT YET

Today, more and more pregnancies don't just "happen" but are discussed, agreed on, and planned well in advance of actual conception. For years, my husband and I agreed that when I reached thirty years old, "we" would begin to try to get pregnant, and I know numerous couples who have personal timetables as to when they'll stop using birth control. When you do this kind of preplanning, you are in a unique position: you have the chance to take steps now—prepregnancy—that can increase the likelihood that your baby will be normal and healthy in every way.

The idea of "preconception health" is still very new, but the concept is rooted in the belief that many problems occur before most women even realize they are pregnant, during the earliest weeks of pregnancy. In these weeks, the embryo is in its most rapid stage of development: all the fetal organs are forming and virtually millions of cells are dividing and differentiating. And during this critical stage of fetal growth and development, it's believed that the healthier a mother's body, life-style, and environment are, the lower the risk that something will go wrong.

That isn't to imply that when growing conditions are perfect for a baby from the very first moment of his or her life, you are guaranteed that a perfect baby will be born. Some genetic factors, for instance, may present unavoidable risks or problems. But it does make sense that if you reduce your exposure to hazards and habits proven harmful to a fetus before you conceive, you will, in turn, reduce the chances of a defect or disability. In addition, you can't underestimate how much planning ahead can make for an easier pregnancy psychologically; there is so much less to worry about or brood over when you know you've provided a pristine environment for your unborn baby from day one.

The five steps outlined below steer you away from things that might be harmful as well as guide you toward practices that create the best conditions for a baby's growth. Don't be discouraged into abandoning them if you don't conceive right away. Even highly fertile young couples take four to eight months on average to conceive once they stop using contraception; couples over thirty-five years old should expect to take longer, about a year or so.

❧ 1. See Your Obstetrician/Gynecologist

Prepregnancy is the best time to get existing medical problems under control, to expose undetected problems, and to pinpoint any aspects of your health or life-style that may be of potential concern during pregnancy. Besides a thorough physical, a checkup should include:

Immunity testing. A blood test can determine if you're immune to rubella (commonly known as German measles), an infection which can cause miscarriage, stillbirth, or serious birth defects. If you're not immune you can get vaccinated, although you then must wait at least three months before trying to conceive. If there's a chance you might be pregnant, immunization is not recommended, since the vaccine itself might be harmful to the developing fetus. Your immune status for toxoplasmosis, an infection transmitted in cat feces and found in raw meat than can cause birth defects and hepatitis B (another virus that puts the fetus at risk), should be checked, too.

A *sexually transmitted disease* (STD) screening. You should be tested for chlamydia, syphillis, and gonorrhea, since these STDs may not cause symptoms yet can lead to miscarriage, premature birth, fetal brain damage, or blindness. You should also be tested for the HIV infection (the virus that causes AIDS) if there is any chance you've been in contact with it.

A *genetic profile.* This is to determine if either you or your partner is from a family or ethnic group that is at high risk for birth defects. Being thirty-five years old or older also puts you at higher risk for genetic problems. Having a genetic profile done before pregnancy can, in some cases, help you avoid problems entirely. For instance, if a woman with the rare, inherited metabolic disorder, phenylketonuria (PKU—if you had this, you would know about it), sticks to a special diet before she conceives, her fetus will be spared mental retardation. But even when a profile can't actually help reduce risks, it may help prepare you to face the odds and to forewarn you about any tough decisions a pregnancy might pose.

Blood pressure check. High blood pressure, which is often symptomless, can cause a variety of pregnancy complications, so it makes sense to detect it and get it under control before conceiving.

Birth-control review. The standard ob/gyn advice to Pill users is to wait until you've had three regular periods before trying to conceive. That's because there is some evidence that the rate of miscarriage is slightly higher in women who conceive just after coming off the Pill. Also, once oral contraceptive use has stopped, it takes some time for ovulation to regain its natural cycle and hormone balance.

IUD-users are generally advised to wait one natural period after the IUD is removed before trying to get pregnant. Users of diaphragms, contraceptive jellies, creams, or foams simply need to stop using these things, preferably after a cycle has been completed—i.e., wait until you get your period, then stop using the diaphragm, contraceptive jelly, cream, or foam.

Breast and pelvic exam. Things like breast lumps, abnormal Pap smears, ovarian cysts, and fibroid tumors are better investigated before pregnancy. Even though some conditions can't necessarily be cleared up, only managed, there is less chance of a serious complication cropping up during pregnancy if you and your doctor have been alerted to a specific problem beforehand.

Medication review. Since many drugs can be harmful to the fetus, you should discuss the safety of all the medications you use, including any over-the-counter ones.

A discussion of work hazards. Certain jobs involve exposure to radiation, chemicals, or other hazards that could be harmful to a developing fetus. A hospital worker, for instance, could come in contact with an infectious disease that might harm her fetus. Talk with your doctor about your job to find out if it is likely to pose any health risk to your pregnancy. (For a more detailed discussion of occupation-related hazards, see pp. 60–63).

❧ 2. Control Your Vices

Unhealthy habits are hard to break at any time, but breaking them can be especially difficult during pregnancy when you're faced with additional physical and psychological pressures. That's why it's safest to stop the following habits prior to pregnancy:

Smoking. Pregnant women who smoke have a greater chance of ectopic pregnancy (see p. 36), vaginal bleeding, miscarriage, stillbirth, preterm birth, and cesarean birth. And, mothers-to-be who smoke have a higher incidence of giving birth to low-birth-weight babies, who tend to be susceptible to a wide range of illnesses and disease.

Drinking. Heavy drinking can cause fetal alcohol syndrome (FAS), a pattern of facial malformations and mental and physical growth impairments. But even moderate social drinking (one to two drinks a day) has been linked to problems in behavior, attention span, and intellectual ability. The U.S. Surgeon General recommends that women who are trying to conceive cut out all drinking, from hard liquor to wine to beer. Some doctors, however, feel that if you limit yourself to an occasional drink while you're trying to conceive, you'll still be on the safe side.

Drug-taking. Even if a woman is only a "recreational user," not an "addict," illicit drugs can make a pernicious assault on an unborn child. Using drugs such as cocaine, crack, heroin, methadone, barbiturates, and amphetamines cannot only cause a wide range of both physical and mental handicaps, but may also force a newborn to suffer the effects of withdrawal at birth. "Lighter" drugs such as marijuana and hashish have also been linked to pregnancy complications and birth defects, although conclusive research on their effects is still limited.

❧ 3. Evaluate Your Environment for Toxic Substances

Toxic substances—such as pollution, lead, or pesticides—can potentially damage a developing fetus. In many cases, specific research on how great a risk a particular toxin poses to a fetus is still very limited. But, in general, it's believed that a) the prenatal effects of many toxic substances are likely to be subtle, manifested not so much in overt physical deformities but in learning and behavioral dysfunctions; and b) when several different toxins are present during a pregnancy, the combined risk is greater than the simple sum of individual threats. In other words, the effect is synergistic: one agent doesn't just add to the risk of another, but multiplies or exaggerates it. So each toxic substance you can eliminate from your life helps decrease the destructiveness of the ones you might not be able to directly control (such as air pollution). Below is a list of potential hazards it makes sense to avoid whenever there's a chance you might be pregnant:

• Garden and yard products, such as pesticides, herbicides, fungicides, and chemical fertilizers
• Arts and crafts materials, namely paint and varnish removers, aerosol sprays, ceramic glazes, silver solder, rubber cement, and airplane glue
• Photography chemicals
• Chemical hair dyes
• Household cleaning products that have strong smelling

fumes, such as oven cleaners (the exceptions are ammonia and chlorine bleach, which are probably safe)
   • Paint strippers, spray paints, and/or anything that contains benzene
   • Lead. Two common sources of exposure to lead are drinking water (older homes often have plumbing systems that contain lead pipes or solder) and paint (although lead-based paints are no longer sold, if you renovate a house that was painted with lead-based paint you may inhale the particles)
   • X-rays, including dental ones, unless they are absolutely necessary. If an X-ray is recommended, always find out first if there are any alternative ways to make a diagnosis: can ultra-sound, for example, be used, since it doesn't involve radiation? If you must be X-rayed, find out if you can shield your abdomen by wearing a lead apron and request that the lowest level of radiation possible be used.

≿ 4. Review Your Eating Habits

The fetus needs high-quality food energy to develop properly; without good nutrition its growth can be impaired. So it makes sense to review the following three aspects of your diet prepregnancy.

Your weight. Being either overweight or underweight can complicate your pregnancy.

Overweight expectant mothers are more prone to high blood pressure, diabetes, and are at higher risk for having a cesarean birth. Yet pregnancy is not the time for an overweight woman to try to diet, since doing so could cheat her unborn baby of an adequate nutrient supply. Underweight mothers-to-be often have a difficult time consuming enough food to get all the nutrients necessary for proper fetal development and so tend to be more susceptible to having below-normal birth-weight babies. These smaller babies are frequently more vulnerable to illness than normal-weight ones.

Obviously, to be well nourished and to achieve a healthy weight (by either losing or gaining) before conceiving is the safest, surest way to avoid weight-related pregnancy problems.

Your food intake. Fetal growth is dependent on the fuel you provide, which is why eating a balanced diet is so important. Eating wisely, in general, means eating plenty of fresh fruits and vegetables; choosing whole-grain products over refined ones; including lean meats, poultry, and fish in your diet regularly; and consuming several servings of dairy foods such as yogurt, milk, and cheese everyday. Unless you regularly skip meals and survive on fast and processed foods, a healthy prepregnancy diet shouldn't be all that difficult to achieve.

Your supplement habit. Extra or megadoses of vitamins and minerals can be toxic to a fetus and in some cases may even cause birth defects. On the other hand, taking a normal dose multi-vitamin/multimineral supplement (one that sticks to the Recommended Daily Allowances or is specially formulated for prenatal use) may be a wise idea. There is evidence that multivitamins, when taken in the early weeks of pregnancy, may help reduce the risk of neural-tube defects (defects of the brain and/or spinal cord), which are often fatal.

HEALTH INSURANCE ALERT

Most insurance policies have "preexisting-condition limitation" clauses. These clauses exclude you from receiving benefits for medical conditions that started before the contract's effective date or that started before a certain waiting period. For example, most basic Blue Cross/Blue Shield plans will only cover a pregnancy after you've been enrolled in the plan for at least eleven months. Almost no insurance policy will cover a pregnancy that commences on or before the contract's starting date. In addition, a surprisingly large number of health insurance contracts won't provide any benefits at all for a "normal pregnancy." So even if you have had insurance coverage for several years, it pays to review your policy before getting pregnant.

ба   *SELECTING THE SEX OF YOUR BABY*   ба

Although there has been considerable research into the question of gender selection, there is still no foolproof method for determining the sex of a baby before conception. There are, however, two approaches which claim to have success rates as high as 80 percent.

One technique, patented by a company called Gametrics Limited, involves separating X-chromosome-bearing sperm (which produce a girl) from Y-chromosome-bearing ones (which produce a boy), then artificially inseminating the sperm of the desired sex. The procedure is used at fifty medical centers in the United States. To find out more about the technique and where it is performed, you can send a stamped, self-addressed envelope to Gametrics Limited, P.O. Box 68, Alzada, MT 59311.

The other method involves carefully timing intercourse and regulating the acidity/alkalinity of the vagina. Making love two to twenty-four hours before ovulation and douching with two tablespoons of baking soda diluted in one quart of water beforehand is supposed to favor a boy; making love thirty-six hours before ovulation and douching with two tablespoons vinegar diluted in one quart water beforehand is supposed to favor a girl. The formula, developed by Dr. Landrum B. Shettles and detailed in his book *How to Choose the Sex of Your Baby* (New York: Doubleday, 1989), attempts to manipulate the fact that X- and Y-chromosome–bearing sperm seem to have different weights and travel at different speeds.

The majority of ob-gyns doubt that these techniques can actually deliver the success rates they claim. And according to American Fertility Society statements, no current technique for determining sex provides a reasonable assurance of success. Still, as long as it's understood that there are no guarantees, there is no reason to believe that trying either method does any harm.

❧ 5. Exercise Moderately

Whenever there's a possibility that you might be pregnant, you'll want to avoid increasing either the amount or intensity of vigorous exercise that you normally do. When you overexert yourself there's the chance that your body temperature may rise; elevated maternal body temperatures during the early weeks of gestation have been associated in animal studies with fetal central-nervous-system defects. So far, though, all the evidence seems to indicate that as long as you're not starting a vigorous regime but are sticking to a workout you are well accustomed to, continuing to exercise is safe for most normal, healthy women both before and during pregnancy.

2

MONTH ONE

(0 TO 4½ WEEKS)

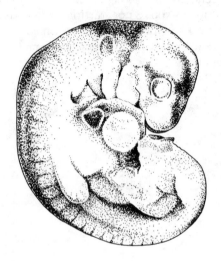

?♣ *Your Baby*

WEIGHT: less than ⅓ of an ounce
LENGTH: ¼ to ½ inches

During this month, the speed and number of developments that take place are remarkable.

At the time of fertilization, one sperm meets with the egg in your fallopian tube. If the sperm that penetrates the egg carries a Y chromosome, a boy is conceived; if the sperm carries an X chromosome, a girl.

Just a few hours after fertilization, the first cell division takes place, the first division of literally billions that must occur before your baby is full formed. After about a week of travel down the fallopian tube, the fertilized egg reaches your uterus or womb, where it burrows into the lining, attaches itself, and then begins to grow at an astounding rate.

By the third week, the embryo's brain starts to take shape, and a primitive heart begins to pump and circulate blood. Less than a week and a half later, the blueprint for every major organ and tissue is laid down. The structure that eventually develops into your baby's backbone, skull, and ribs sprouts into being as do the beginnings of the stomach, liver, kidneys, and nervous and musculature systems.

In just one month's time, then, the fertilized egg transforms itself from two microscopic cells into a living embryo with a beating heart. Although it's no bigger than a pea and looks like a tiny fish, the embryo is almost fifty times the size it was when it started life four and a half weeks ago.

❧ Your Body

NORMAL BODY CHANGES

Your entire body adjusts to meet the demands of pregnancy, although the changes in your reproductive organs are the most impressive.

At the start of pregnancy, your uterus is an organ that is approximately three inches long, two inches wide, and one inch deep. By the end of the ninth month, it is twelve to fourteen inches long, eight to ten inches wide, and eight to nine inches deep. Its weight increases from two ounces to almost two pounds. The uterus enlarges this dramatically so that it can contain a seven- to nine-pound baby (on average), the placenta, an umbilical cord, and amniotic fluid.

By the fourth week of pregnancy, thin, papery membranes form a sac within the uterus. This sac fills with a liquid, called amniotic fluid, which envelopes the embryo and cushions it so it's protected from the impact of any direct blows or jolts to your abdomen.

Also forming inside the uterus is the placenta. This is a flat, disc-shaped structure that's attached to your uterus on the one side and to the umbilical cord on the other. The placenta serves

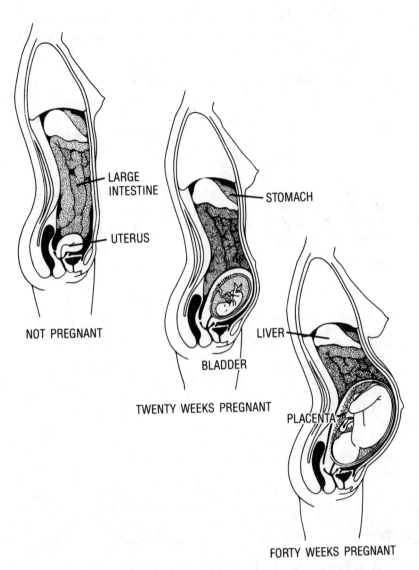

LARGE
INTESTINE

STOMACH

UTERUS

NOT PREGNANT

LIVER

BLADDER

TWENTY WEEKS PREGNANT

PLACENTA

FORTY WEEKS PREGNANT

As pregnancy progresses, the growing fetus and expanding uterus begin to crowd your large intestine, liver, and stomach. Some women find this makes them more prone to constipation, heartburn, or upper abdominal pains (see "Common Side Effects of Late Pregnancy," p. 112).

primarily as a nutrition station, sending protective antibodies, oxygen, and nutrients from your body to the fetus, via the umbilical cord. It also produces hormones. By the end of the ninth month, the placenta measures about six to eight inches around and weighs about one and a half pounds. It's what is commonly called the "afterbirth."

Other organs or body systems that will change over the next nine months:

Your *cervix* softens and shortens toward the end of pregnancy, partly in preparation for labor, when it must thin (efface) and enlarge (dilate) to allow the baby to pass through.

Your *fallopian tubes and ovaries* shift in position, moving upward into your abdomen as your uterus expands.

Your *vagina and vulva* get ready for the tremendous stretching of childbirth—the connective tissues and muscles distend, loosen, and lengthen. To help promote these changes, the blood supply to your vagina and vulva greatly increases, making these organs become slightly bluish or purplish in color. In addition, your vaginal secretions (leukorrhea) may become more noticeable, especially in the later months of pregnancy (even warranting frequent underwear changes), plus your vaginal tissue may feel more "congested," full, and prickly, especially during and after lovemaking.

Your *joints*, particularly those in your pelvic region, loosen, slacken, and relax as they prepare for the "parting" or spreading of childbirth.

❧ FIGURING YOUR DUE DATE ❧

To figure your due date yourself (most doctors will do it for you on your first visit), simply subtract three months and then add seven days to the first day of your last menstrual period. Or, count ahead 280 days from the first day of your last period. It's estimated that only 10 to 20 percent of all women deliver on their exact due date. Also, it's normal for babies to arrive two weeks earlier or two weeks later than planned. Due-date calculations, then, are not foolproof formulas; they simply provide you with a loose guess as to when you might deliver.

Your *blood volume,* in order to meet the increased needs of your enlarging organs, increases threefold. This means your heart must pump harder (which is not a problem for a healthy heart). As a result, you may be short of breath at times. This increase in blood volume is also responsible for one of pregnancy's best side effects—a facial flush or "glow" that usually becomes apparent by the end of the third month.

❧ Your Doctor Appointment

CHOOSING A CAREGIVER

Pregnancy is a time when intimate questions, little fears, and/or nagging worries sometimes crop up. To ensure your peace of mind, choose a caregiver whom you trust and respect. You want someone you feel comfortable speaking with, no matter how "silly" your concern might be.

But choosing who will help guide you through pregnancy is not a decision that can be made in isolation. It needs to be made in concert with another major consideration: where you want to have your baby. The two are a package deal. Once you've picked your obstetrician, for instance, you have automatically picked the hospital he or she practices out of, too.

There are no hard-and-fast rules on whether it makes sense to shop for a caretaker or delivery spot first—it all depends on what is most important to you. (For example, if giving birth in a homelike environment is a high priority, then you'll want to find a maternity center or hospital with birthing rooms, first; a midwife or doctor who practices there, second.)

The discussion ahead—"Obstetrician or Midwife?" and the chart "Where Should You Have Your Baby?"—should help you sort out your priorities, and steer you to the option likely to be best for you.

OBSTETRICIAN OR MIDWIFE?

You may have a third option in your community, too: a family practitioner (FP), who may be trained to provide prenatal care and to do normal deliveries. The advantage of an FP is that he or she is not only able to care for you but for your newborn and other family members, too, making a particularly close, ongoing relationship possible. But should any serious problems develop during your pregnancy or during childbirth, an FP is usually not equipped to handle them; he or she will then refer you to an obstetrician or other specialist.

Obstetrician

Credentials. An obstetrician (OB) is an M.D. who has had additional specialty training in obstetrics and gynecology.

Type of care provided. An obstetrician is equipped to deal with almost all problems that may arise during pregnancy or childbirth. An obstetrician, for example, may perform genetic tests, dilation and curettage (cleaning of the uterus) after a miscarriage, and cesarean sections, since he or she is trained in surgical procedures.

Potential advantages. Since an obstetrician can conduct any special tests you might need and can come to your aid if any complications arise, you are assured continuity of care (something that can be very valuable emotionally if a problem does crop up). In most areas of the country, obstetricians are plentiful and easy to find (in fact, almost 95 percent of births in the U.S. are supervised by these doctors). Given that there is a relatively large pool of obstetricians to choose from, it's likely you can find one who has a manner, style, and perspective you like and trust.

Potential disadvantages. Although there are still obstetricians who take a "Doctor knows best, so just do as I say" attitude, if you shop around you can probably sidestep this potential problem and find one who is willing to be more of a partner during your pregnancy.

Most obstetricians tend to deliver in hospitals, so you may find it virtually impossible to find one who will agree to attend a home birth. Also, as a group, obstetricians tend to favor the use of technology and intervention in pregnancy. So if you feel very strongly about *not* having a certain medical procedure, you should be sure to voice your feelings before your pregnancy advances very far. Then, if there is a basic difference in opinion, you still have plenty of time to switch to another caregiver.

Type of practice. An obstetrician may have a solo practice, which has one major advantage: you get to see the same person at each prenatal visit. It also has one major potential disadvantage: if he or she is on vacation when you go into labor, someone other than your primary obstetrician (a backup person you probably will have met at least once) will deliver your baby.

An obstetrician may work in a partnership, which means you'll alternate appointments with each partner during your nine months. If you like both partners, this arrangement can be ideal, since you'll know both doctors quite well by the time you are ready to deliver. Or an obstetrician may work in a group or be part of a health maintenance organization (HMO). If the group is big, the potential drawback is that you may not be able to establish a close, continuous relationship with just one physician. On the plus side, you'll be privy to a greater range of expertise and advice.

Finding a referral. If you can't find an obstetrician through recommendations from like-minded friends or family, your family practitioner, local hospital, or local medical society should be able to supply you with names.

Certified Nurse-Midwife (CNM)

Credentials. A CNM is a registered nurse with advanced education in clinical midwifery, normal obstetrics/gynecology, and newborn care. There are approximately thirty-three hundred CNMs practicing in the U.S. A CNM should not be confused with a lay midwife, who is usually self-taught, has no standard training or certification, and may not legally practice in most states.

Type of care provided. Considered specialists in *normal* prenatal care, CNMs are required to have a backup physician who can step in, during labor and delivery, if problems arise. Most studies show that a woman experiencing a healthy pregnancy is as safe in the hands of a CNM as she would be in the hands of a physician. But because nurse-midwives are only expert in "normal" or low-risk pregnancy, that means not every woman can take advantage of a CNM's services. Competent CNMs will refuse to take on your pregnancy if you have any of the following factors that put you at high risk for complications: bleeding during pregnancy, history of previous miscarriages or difficult births, diabetes, hypertension, Rh-sensitization, and/or an incompetent cervix. Also, some CNMs tend to prefer not to work with first-time mothers who are between the ages of thirty-five and forty-five.

Potential advantages. A CNM may be more generous with her time at checkups and may be more apt to stay at your side, coaching and encouraging you throughout labor, than an obstetrician. She may also provide more emotional support and psychological care, especially in the postpartum period. A CNM may actually come to your home to give you advice on breast-feeding and baby care several times in the weeks after birth. For many women, the biggest draw of a CNM is her "noninterventionist attitude" and the fact that, since she has very limited surgical training, she cannot perform a cesarean section. In other words, many women feel that in choosing a CNM, they reduce their risk of an unnecessary c-section.

In addition, if your birth is normal, you may be able to reap significant savings by using a CNM, since these fees tend to be much lower than obstetrician's fees.

Potential disadvantages. CNMs are only equipped to deal with normal, low-risk situations, not with complications. In the early stages of pregnancy, that means your CNM may not be able to really help you if you experience bleeding, cramping, or a miscarriage; she may only be able to refer you to the local emergency room.

Later in a pregnancy, there's about a 20 percent chance that some complication will arise making it impossible for your midwife to deliver your baby. So although many women choose a CNM because they want to give birth in a nonhospital setting, one out of five will end up delivering in a hospital under the care of a doctor. And if this happens, there is the chance that you could end up spending more for the services of a CNM than you would have for those of an obstetrician.

Type of practice. CNMs usually work in groups, out of a maternity center or hospital birthing facility, with physicians on call. In other words, doctors don't routinely care for or see patients; they are simply ready to step in if complications arise. (Be sure to get information about the background credentials and availability of a CNM's backup physician. Also, find out how and where medical tests like amniocentesis are performed and how much extra they cost.)

Less frequently, midwives work out of a doctor's office as part of a group practice that includes one or more obstetricians. In that case, you'll usually get to know the doctors, too, since your appointments will rotate among members of the group.

Finding a Referral. To locate a practicing certified nurse-midwife in your area, you can get names by writing to the American College of Nurse-Midwives, 1522 K Street, N.W., Suite 1120, Washington, DC 20005.

Fees. CNM fees range from $600 to $2,000, the higher end of the scale tending to include more services—such as childbirth education, nutrition counseling, and postpartum house calls—per dollar spent than physicians' fees. If your birth is normal, you may be able to reap significant savings compared to a typical obstetrician-directed hospital birth. But if you run into complications, you can end up spending more for a CNM's services since you may not only have to pay the CNM and maternity center but a doctor and a hospital as well. Most insurance policies cover certified nurse-midwife fees.

Where Should You Have Your Baby?

	Setting	Potential Pros	Potential Cons	Questions to Ask
Hospital	Maternity wards usually comprise a series of undecorated, specially designated rooms; there are rooms for labor, rooms for delivery, rooms for recovery; rooms for the postpartum stay; and a nursery. You are transferred from room to room as your labor progresses.	You have instant access to a pediatrician and anesthesiologist as well as to an obstetrician if unforeseen complications arise. Although hospital delivery is the most expensive option, generally your insurance policy will reimburse you for the majority of charges.	The high-tech atmosphere of the hospital may make you feel you have no control. Often there are strict rules on what position you must labor and deliver in, when you can nurse and see your baby, how long you must stay, and so on.	To get information about a hospital's labor and delivery policies, you can take a hospital tour (just call the public relations department to arrange it). If you've already chosen your doctor or CNM, ask him or her. Questions to ask: Can your partner be with you throughout labor and delivery? Is fetal monitoring and intravenous hookup mandatory? What is the cesarean-section rate? (the national average is 21 percent). What are the nursery rules, length-of-stay regulations, and visiting regulations?
Hospital-based Family Birth Rooms (FBRs)	These usually have more homey elements—curtains, showers, cushioned chairs, wallpaper— than standard hospital rooms. You labor, deliver, and recover in the same room.	You have the comfort of a warm, intimate environment, plus the comfort of knowing that a full array of medical experts and technology is right at hand if needed. Costs are generally the same as for a hospital.	Hospitals with FBRs may be hard to find. You may be transferred to the hospital's standard labor/delivery setting if a problem arises or, in some cases, you may be excluded from using the FBRs because all of them are already in use.	What percentage of patients who sign up to use an FBR actually end up using it? What are the circumstances in which you would not be able to use the FBR? What are the nursery, length-of-stay, and visiting policies?
Freestanding Maternity Center (FMC)	This is a birthing center that is not attached to a hospital's facilities; there are approximately 135 of them in the U.S. They usually have lounges, living rooms, kitchens, informal examining rooms, and birthing rooms that look like bedrooms. Costs are generally much lower than a hospital's.	Ambience is homelike, relaxed, yet offers many of the safety features such as lifesaving equipment and obstetricians-on-call that a hospital would. Generally, you can walk around, eat, and bathe during labor. You usually have a free choice of delivery positions. You're not separated from your baby after birth.	There's at least a 20 percent chance (the average chance a low-risk woman has of developing problems) that you'll be transferred to a hospital. Release from an FMC is usually twelve hours after birth, which may not be enough time for a new, first-time mother to recover and adjust.	Is the facility accredited by the Commission for the Accreditation of Freestanding Birth Centers? What percentage of patients actually give birth at the center? What are the arrangements if you need to be transferred to a hospital? How swiftly can you expect to be transferred; what hospital will you go to; will your CNM accompany you; and will a pediatrician and obstetrician be quickly available? For more information about FMCs and for help in locating one near you, send a stamped, self-

Setting	Potential Pros	Potential Cons	Questions to Ask
			addressed envelope to the National Association of Childbearing Centers, RD 1, Box 1, Perkiomenville, PA 18074.
Home	Whatever yours happens to look like.	Setting is familiar; no restrictions on who may be present at the birth; no risk of technology being forced on you; you're not separated from your baby after birth. The only cost is the attending physician's or midwife's fee.	The American College of Obstetricians and Gynecologists and the American Academy of Pediatrics strongly oppose home births. Their chief worry is safety. In an unexpected emergency, a home setting simply doesn't offer quick access to experts or medical equipment. Also, finding a physician or midwife to attend a home birth can be difficult.	Does the prenatal program include several home visits to ensure your house is properly set up and supplied for labor, delivery, and newborn care? For more information about home birth you can contact an organization that publishes numerous pamphlets on home birth: The International Childbirth Education Association, P.O. Box 20048, Minneapolis, MN 55420-0048; 800-624-4934.

❧ Your Diet

FOODS TO EAT

The fetus depends on you to provide the right mix of vitamins, minerals, and calories so that he or she can develop properly. You need to eat a healthy diet, in other words, so your baby-to-be can grow strong and healthy. It's as simple as that.

A balanced pregnancy diet isn't difficult to achieve. Strict calorie counting and portion-sizing are not necessary. If your diet is more or less healthy now, you'll probably find you only need to make minor changes in the way you eat. These changes are likely to consist of increasing your intake of certain foods, since you do need a variety of extra vitamins and minerals as well as extra calories.

The nine guidelines that follow distill the wealth of detailed scientific information on pregnancy nutrition and turn it into an easy-to-follow general eating plan. The guidelines take into account that you need to gain weight during pregnancy, yet help you avoid gaining to excess (for a full discussion of how much you'll need to gain, see pp. 53–55).

1. Drink a quart of milk a day. This may be the biggest dietary challenge you'll face. But getting an adequate supply of the mineral calcium—twelve hundred milligrams daily, which is what a quart of milk provides—is essential for the healthy formation of your baby's skeletal system as well as for his or her future teeth.

Calcium is important for your future health, too. If your intake is low, calcium will be withdrawn from your bones to supply the baby. This bone loss may never be fully recovered after pregnancy, making you far more prone later in life to osteoporosis (the condition in which your bones deteriorate, becoming brittle and easily broken).

Skim and low-fat milk give you the least calories and fat in exchange for fulfilling your calcium needs. If you have difficulty digesting milk, you can try Lactaid milk, available in most grocery stores, or acidophilus milk, found in health-food stores. Both have reduced amounts of the milk sugar lactose, the substance that some find hard to digest. (For information on calcium-rich alternatives to milk, see pp. 103–04.)

2. Eat a meat, fish, or chicken meal most days of the week. This is likely to provide you with enough protein, which is critical for building fetal tissue, manufacturing hormones, meeting energy needs, and preventing hypertension late in pregnancy.

Meeting the increased protein needs of pregnancy (requirements almost double, going up from about forty-five grams to seventy-five grams) takes virtually no thought for most women. That's because most Americans already eat twice the protein they need a day. In other words, you probably already eat the amount of protein you need everyday for pregnancy.

You need to eat, most days of the week, four ounces of beef, veal, pork, chicken, turkey, shrimp, or salmon. That, in addition to your daily quart of milk (which is rich in protein), will take care of your pregnancy protein requirements. Even if you substitute meals based on foods like eggs, rice and beans, pasta with vegetables and cheese, or stir fries with tofu for meals based on meat a few times a week, you should still get an adequate supply of protein.

However, if you are a vegetarian, you cannot afford to be quite so casual about meeting your protein needs; as long as you include dairy products, though, it is possible to get enough protein. (See "Meeting Protein Needs without Meat," pp. 90–93.)

3. Include a complex carbohydrate at every meal. Complex carbohydrates have a high concentration of B vitamins, which the fetus needs in order to produce healthy red blood cells and nerves. Complex carbohydrates also provide fiber, which helps food pass easily through your digestive system. Pick one of the complex carbohydrates listed below at each meal:

Black-eyed peas
Corn or bran muffins
Corn tortillas
Egg noodles
Kasha
Kidney beans
Lentils
Macaroni
Pasta
Peas
Pinto beans
Rice
Rye or pumpernickel bread
Soybeans
Sweet potatoes or yams (with skin)
White potatoes (with skin)
Whole-grain breakfast cereal (such as Nutri-Grain wheat, Wheaties, Wheat Chex, Total, puffed wheat, shredded wheat, oatmeal, raisin bran, cornflakes)
Whole-grain crackers
Whole-wheat or -grain bread

4. Eat something dark green every day. Dark-green vegetables are invariably nutritious, providing either ample amounts of vitamin A (which is important for reducing your susceptibility to infection), vitamin C (necessary for the healthy development of the fetus's bones, muscles, and cartilage), or folic acid (essential for the formation of the baby's central nervous system).

Try to vary your choices from the list below, and to eat big helpings (at least half a cup):

Asparagus
Broccoli
Brussels sprouts
Chicory
Collard greens
Escarole
Green peppers
Kale
Mustard greens
Red- or green-leaf lettuce
Romaine lettuce
Snow peas
Spinach
Swiss chard
Watercress

5. Eat at least three different fruits or vegetables a day. When you include a lot of different fruits and vegetables in your diet, it becomes easy to get the variety of vitamins and minerals you need. Choose at least two of the fruits and at least one vegetable listed below. Always wash produce carefully before eating to eliminate pesticide residues.

Vegetables	Fruits	
Artichokes	Apples	Peaches
Avocados	Apricots	Papaya
Beets	Bananas	Pears
Cabbage	Blueberries	Pineapples
Carrots	Cantaloupe	Plums

Vegetables	Fruits	
Cauliflower	Cherries	Raspberries
Corn	Cranberries	Strawberries
Eggplant	Grapefruit	
Kohlrabi	Grapes	
Red peppers	Mangoes	
Squash	Nectarines	
Tomatoes	Oranges	
Turnips		

6. Limit sweets, fats, and junk food. Indulging a sweet tooth or succumbing to a junk-food craving now and then won't harm you or the baby. But a steady diet of foods that are not very nutritious (such as cakes, pastries, candy bars, doughnuts, potato chips, french fries) shortchanges the fetus of a healthy, varied supply of vitamins and minerals. Besides, a pregnant woman only needs about three hundred to five hundred extra calories a day, so when you eat lots of high-calorie sweets or junk foods you end up putting on much more weight than is necessary for your or your baby's good health.

7. Salt. Salt requirements rise during pregnancy. However, there's no need to go overboard and to oversalt foods. If you follow the dictates of your taste buds, your sodium needs will almost certainly be met.

8. Drink six to eight glasses of water a day. You need this much liquid (about forty-eight to sixty-four ounces a day) to supply the rise in body fluids you experience during pregnancy and to prevent constipation. Substituting unsweetened fruit or vegetable juice for a glass or two of water can make meeting your daily liquid quota easier and more palatable.

9. Take the vitamin/mineral supplement prescribed by your doctor. This should be primarily high in iron and folic acid, two minerals that are hard to get enough of no matter how well you eat.

Since iron-containing supplements may aggravate an already upset stomach, many doctors advise you to wait to use supplements until after your third month of pregnancy, when the danger of morning sickness has usually passed.

FOOD AND DRINK TO AVOID

If it isn't pesticide residues on fruits and vegetables, then it's hormones and antibiotics in beef and chicken. These days, virtually everything edible can start to seem like a threat to your health.

Yet you must eat. So rather than catalog every general concern regarding the safety of our food supply, the list below concentrates on documented dangers that are possible to avoid.

Raw eggs. The bacteria salmonella thrives in raw and undercooked eggs and can cause severe diarrhea and fever (high maternal fevers can cause birth defects). Avoid Caesar salads, eggnog, hollandaise sauce, and homemade mayonnaise, which are frequently made with raw eggs, and only eat well-cooked eggs (hard-boiled ones or eggs that have been poached or fried for several minutes).

Raw fish or meat. Raw meat can transmit toxoplasmosis; raw shellfish and fish (such as sushi) can carry any number of parasites.

Freshwater and sport fish. Fish caught in local lakes and rivers (such as trout, perch, catfish, bluegill, crappie, etc.) carry a high risk of being contaminated with pesticides, heavy metals, and cancer-causing chemicals like PCBs. What actual risk these polluted fish might pose to the developing fetus isn't known, but it's generally thought safest to stick to freshwater fish that has been produced on a commercial ranch (most market-sold catfish and rainbow trout, for instance, are farmed). Smaller open-ocean fish, like flounder and sole, may also be safer than larger open-ocean fish, such as tuna and swordfish, which live longer and have more time to accumulate toxic metals like mercury in their flesh. As an additional precaution, it's best to limit yourself to one fish meal a week and to vary the type you choose, so you're not always eating the same fish from the same area.

Coffee, teas, or colas in excess. Although recent studies have failed to establish a relationship between caffeine intake and birth defects, low birth weight, and/or premature birth, fears about the dangers of caffeine during pregnancy still linger in certain sectors of the medical and general community. This is partly because preliminary studies performed several years ago found that pregnant lab rats who were fed extremely high doses of caffeine gave birth to abnormal offspring. "Just in case," the Food and Drug Administration still recommends that pregnant women consume no more than two to three cups of caffeinated coffee, cola, or tea a day. As for caffeine-free diet sodas that contain NutraSweet®, studies to date have found no harmful effects on the developing fetus at normal doses (as long as the mother-to-be does not have the rare inherited metabolic disorder called phenylketonuria [PKU]—if you had this disorder, you would have been on an extremely restricted diet from birth to adolescence).

Your water? Water pipes in the homes of millions of Americans contain lead, a harmful metal that has been proven to cause neurological damage in fetuses that are continually exposed to it. The problem is most likely to exist in homes built before 1930 (when lead piping was the norm) or in homes built prior to 1986 that have copper plumbing (in which lead solder was usually used). Although letting your water run for a few minutes before using it helps flush out the lead, if you suspect there is lead in your plumbing system, you probably should consider having the lead content of your water tested. Your local water department will often do testing for you free of charge.

Drinking water in some areas may also contain low levels of environmental contaminants (industrial chemicals, solvents, or metals). Although the effects of fetal exposure to this kind of tainted drinking water has not been researched, it may make sense to take a few precautionary measures. If you're not sure your water supply is safe, find out more about it by contacting your local water utility and health departments. Other agencies that can provide information include state departments of public health or environmental engineering, and the regional offices of the Environmental Protection Agency. For answers to general questions about water safety, you can also call the Safe Drinking Water Hotline, at 1-800-426-4791.

ᐧᑍ *Your Workout*

SAFE EXERCISE STANDARDS

Research on exercise during pregnancy is in the fledgling stage, which means doctors still don't know or agree on how much is just right. For example, ask several doctors whether jogging forty-five minutes a day is advisable, and chances are you'll get several conflicting answers.

What is agreed upon at this stage is that moderate amounts of exercise seem to be safe—if a pregnancy is without complications. It may even confer some benefits. Not that exercise will improve the outcome of a pregnancy; studies so far simply don't support the contention that sticking to a workout regime results in fewer unforeseen problems or bigger, healthier babies. But women who remain active do seem to benefit in other ways.

Women who exercise regularly tend to be less plagued by common pregnancy complaints like backache, leg cramps, varicose veins, and constipation. They also seem to have a more positive body image than non-exercisers, especially later in pregnancy when the extra weight begins to show. Exercising also seems to give women a higher tolerance for pain during labor and delivery. Studies point to a postpartum benefit, too: women who stay in shape tend to bounce back to normal activity and energy levels much more quickly after delivery (typically ten days earlier) than women who have been inactive.

The American College of Obstetricians and Gynecologists (ACOG) has developed a set of safe exercise standards that are intended to apply to all pregnant women at all fitness levels. That means that even if you haven't exercised before pregnancy, you can safely follow the guidelines as long as you increase your activity level gradually. On the other hand, if you're entering pregnancy ultrafit, chances are you'll find the ACOG guidelines too restrictive (many experts also find the ACOG rules overly conservative; see "The Vigorous Exercise Debate," pp. 57–58).

The ACOG Exercise Rules

1. You should get your doctor's okay before starting or continuing a fitness regime during pregnancy. In general, you'll be advised against any exercise if you have a history of three or more spontaneous abortions, ruptured membranes, premature labor, bleeding, a diagnosis of placenta previa, an incompetent cervix, cardiac disease, or a multiple pregnancy. If you have high blood pressure, anemia, thyroid disease, diabetes, a history of precipitous labor, intrauterine growth retardation, bleeding during the present pregnancy, or are excessively over- or underweight, you'll generally be advised to avoid *vigorous* exercise and to only work out under the close supervision of your doctor.

2. Limit strenuous exercise—meaning a pulse rate above 140 beats per minute—to fifteen minutes at a time (but you can rest for a half hour, then do another fifteen minutes). An easy way to check your pulse rate: at the peak of your workout, count the pulses in your wrist for fifteen seconds, then multiply by four.

3. Do not let your body temperature rise above 100° F (38° C); check by taking your temperature (use a digital thermometer for a fast, accurate reading) before and immediately after your routine.

4. To reduce your risk of injury, avoid jerky, bouncy movements (such as those in high-impact aerobics), deep extension of joints (such as deep lunges), or stretches during calisthenics.

5. Precede all exercise by at least five minutes of warm-ups; follow it with five to ten minutes of cool-downs.

6. Never ignore the signs of overdoing it—feeling tired, weak, or faint. Stop and rest.

7. If you get thirsty, take a drink break; always drink generous amounts of water both before and after exercise to prevent dehydration. If it's hot and humid, take the day off from exercising. Sweat can't evaporate and cool you down properly in such weather.

8. After the fourth month, don't exercise lying flat on your back, since your expanding uterus may compress the vena cava, the vein that carries blood back to your heart. This could interfere with normal blood flow to the uterus.

9. Stop working out until you see your doctor if any of the following warning signs or symptoms crop up: pain, bleeding,

dizziness, shortness of breath, palpitations, faintness, back pain, pubic pain, difficulty in walking, or tachycardia (abnormally rapid heartbeat after exercising).

Workouts Fit—and Not Fit—for Two

Below is a rundown of the sports and activities that experts feel are safe to continue throughout pregnancy, plus those that should be avoided.

Walking. The ideal exercise, especially if you have been sedentary before pregnancy. Start slowly, then gradually work your way up to a pace of about three or four miles per hour.

Swimming. Improves endurance, and conditions the muscles of your entire body with the advantage of weightlessness, i.e., you don't have the stress of supporting your body weight. Even if you weren't swimming before pregnancy, most doctors feel a moderate program of laps can safely be initiated. But excessively cold or hot water and diving (which could cause trauma to the abdomen) are to be avoided.

Biking. Because it's not a weight-bearing exercise, most physicians feel it's okay to start biking once pregnant. But after the second trimester, when your center of balance begins to shift, a stationary bicycle is generally considered safer.

Jogging. Only if you went into pregnancy a jogger should you consider it. As long as you stop when you begin to feel uncomfortable and are careful not to get overheated, you can safely jog right up to the time of delivery.

Aerobics. ACOG frowns on high-impact workouts, but okays low-impact aerobics. Still, by the third trimester, your added weight may strain your knees and back as well as test your agility and balance during low-impact routines.

Racquet sports. As long as you're an experienced player, tennis, squash, badminton, etc., are safe to play. However, most women find they want to stop playing by the sixth month, when quick lateral moves, running backward, and serving with a well-arched back simply become too awkward and uncomfortable.

Weight training. Recommended, if it's low weight, high repetitions. The worry behind lifting heavy weights: it's thought that if you don't inhale and exhale properly during strenuous lifting blood flow to the baby might be compromised.

Scuba diving. Experienced pregnant divers may continue making very conservative dives—not below thirty-three feet—and limiting dive times to thirty minutes or less. Deeper or longer dives may cause you to experience decompression sickness and cause your baby to suffer a nitrogen imbalance.

Waterskiing. Because high-speed falls may cause forceful entry of water into the vagina, possibly precipitating a miscarriage or premature labor, it should be avoided during pregnancy.

Contact sports. Field hockey, football, basketball, volleyball, and horseback riding are generally not considered safe during pregnancy because of the possibility that your stomach might be struck (by the ball or a fall) with high impact.

Skiing. ACOG advises you to stick to safe slopes so you don't risk sustaining serious falls or injuries (which could put you in bed for a long stretch—a highly uncomfortable situation to be in while pregnant). Also, skiing at altitudes above ten thousand feet is not recommended because of the decreased oxygen supply at those elevations.

The Fitness Rule for All

Every pregnancy is different and women often respond quite differently to the same physical demands. Some women feel capable of exercising at peak levels right up until the time of delivery, while others find they must cut back or even quit. At this point, experts don't know why there is such huge variability among women. But doctors offer this strong advice: listen to your body signals and don't try to "push through" a workout. Instead, be flexible and open to the possibility that you may simply be too tired at times to exercise. Remember, too, that a fitness regime should make you feel better and be comfortable to do—if it is painful or wears you out, the sensible and safe thing to do is to stop.

❧ *Your Feelings*

ENTERING NEW EMOTIONAL TERRITORY

Pregnancy is often billed as a time of calm bliss, a period in which you daydream and relax. Yet for many women, the pregnancy months are turbulent ones—punctuated by anxiety, am-

---

❧   *PRENATAL EXERCISE PROGRAMS*   ❧

Today, prenatal exercise programs are offered at hospitals, YMCAs, private gyms, and dance and aerobic studios. Besides the workout you get, these classes provide you with the opportunity to meet other pregnant women. Especially if you're more or less "isolated" in your pregnancy (you're not surrounded by lots of pregnant friends, relatives, or new moms), an exercise class can serve as an invaluable support group and reference source.

Most programs emphasize stretching, strengthening, and low-impact routines, although some also incorporate swimming and weight lifting. When picking a program, find out what qualifications the instructor has to teach pregnant women: has she been specially trained and tested in prenatal exercise? When participating in a class, make sure the instructor is sensitive to your personal tolerance and comfort level (in other words, be sure she doesn't try to push you past your limits). Also, a good instructor will pay special attention to posture, will include lots of exercises to improve lower-back strength, and will generally be open and patient about answering questions.

bivalence, even existential questioning. Not that there aren't stretches of deep serenity and satisfaction. But pregnancy (and its obvious implication of impending motherhood) can mark a major new stage of personal development; as such, it's no wonder that it may take some time and some "working out" to adjust to it. You're not alone, in other words, if you don't experience the next nine months as one nonstop "glow." Having mixed feelings and varied thoughts is a common, and psychologically normal, part of most pregnancies.

Reaction to the discovery. Under what circumstances you became pregnant will obviously color your reactions. Especially if you had trouble conceiving, you may be surprised by how "earthy" and potent you feel, somehow more womanly, competent, and sexy. If you made an active, conscious decision in concert with your partner to get pregnant, chances are you'll tend to feel proud and joyous as well as more committed to your relationship.

What if you didn't plan this pregnancy? Your feelings may run the gamut from disbelief to despair at not being prepared. But give yourself time: just as most women who start out pregnancy 100 percent enthusiastic usually find that ambivalence creeps in over time, women who initially have negative reactions find they develop acceptance and attachment as their pregnancy progresses.

Mood changes. That hormone levels surge and rage may partly be the reason for the fluctuating moods many women feel in the early months of pregnancy. But the hormone explanation fails to take into account the subtle yet powerful profundity of the pregnancy experience: realizing and accepting that you are actually gestating another person inside your body is an awakening that's bound to have some impact on your emotions and moods.

Feeling mildly depressed, more sensitive, and vulnerable at times are common. Many women also feel more "separate," alone, and introspective; they find they're more absentminded than usual and less interested, for instance, in conversations that they would normally find engaging. This delving into yourself is probably a way of gradually becoming comfortable with your new state of being, your new concept of yourself as a mother. This doesn't mean you will necessarily feel "motherly" or a strong connection to the fetus yet—some women do, others don't.

The "what-if" fears. Almost every woman has them at some point or another, but they tend to be particularly poignant in the first trimester. What if this pregnancy is ectopic? What if the wine I drank before I knew I was pregnant has harmed the baby? What if—insert your fear here—is causing a problem? Surprisingly, many psychologists don't think these kinds of anxieties are entirely negative; instead, they view them as a reflection of your growing attachment to your fetus. Your worries, in other words, show that you're developing a healthy sense of responsibility for your well-being as well as that of your baby.

That doesn't mean you shouldn't try to overcome and alleviate your fears; airing them with your doctor is probably the best way to do that.

Anxieties caused by a previous miscarriage. If you've had a prior pregnancy end in miscarriage, it's natural to experience some emotional fallout in a new pregnancy. Many women find that getting past the week when their previous miscarriage occurred is a major psychological landmark: only when they pass that week can they begin to rest easy in the new pregnancy.

If you've miscarried before, it's not uncommon to find that you constantly monitor your health and the health of the fetus. You may not, for example, be able to resist looking for signs of staining on every trip to the bathroom.

It helps to realize that miscarriages are quite common, and that after one, most women go on to have normal pregnancies (for more on miscarriage see "Pregnancy Loss," pp. 65–71). Also, knowing that it's natural and common to be more nervous this time around can make it easier for you to live with your fears.

﴾ *Your Life-Style*

HABITS AND HOME ACTIVITIES
THAT COULD HARM YOUR BABY

It was once believed that the placenta acted as a barricade to toxins. Today it's known that most drugs, chemicals, and diseases can freely cross the placenta and potentially harm the fetus. Yet many of these hazards are within your control: it's possible, in other words, for you to eliminate your contact with them and thus shield your baby from possible harm.

Cigarette smoking. In essence, when you light up, your baby does, too. Each time you inhale, your womb fills with carbon monoxide, nicotine, tar, resins, and nitrosamines, toxins that dramatically inhibit nutrient and oxygen delivery to your baby while exposing his or her delicate, developing tissue to cancer-causing agents.

The havoc this onslaught can reek on a fetus's health is well documented. It's known, for example, that babies born to smokers tend to be below optimal birth weight and have higher rates of congenital malformations (especially brain damage and cerebral palsy), lower IQ scores, and more learning and behavioral disabilities. It has also been found that the likelihood of death during the first months of life is over 50 percent higher among babies born to mothers who smoke.

In addition, pregnant women who smoke have a greater chance of ectopic pregnancy, vaginal bleeding, miscarriage, stillbirth, premature labor, and *abruptio placentae* (a condition in which the placenta prematurely separates from the uterine wall, necessitating a cesarean section). The safest way to avoid risking your health and your baby's health is to quit instantly upon learning you are pregnant. If you've smoked for many years, however, this might not be realistic. Instead, it may take you a little time to bolster your resolve and conquer your excuses about kicking the habit. If this is the case, you should keep in mind these two goals: First, the less you smoke, the lower your risk, so *cutting down* immediately confers some benefits. Secondly, quitting entirely by the fourth month of your pregnancy greatly reduces the risk of your baby being born prematurely. It seems the maximum amount of damage is done during the last months of pregnancy.

There are many places you can turn to for help, support, and advice about quitting. Local offices of the American Cancer Society, the American Heart Association, and the American Lung Association (listed in your local white pages) often sponsor free stop-smoking clinics as well as provide literature detailing various quitting strategies. There are an array of commercial stop-smoking programs like Smokenders, too (see Smokers Information and Treatment Centers in your yellow pages). And you can always telephone the National Cancer Institute's Health Information Service to find out about other options. The toll-free number is 1-800-4-Cancer.

Drinking. It's been known for a long time that heavy drinking (over six drinks a day) during pregnancy can lead to fetal alcohol syndrome (FAS), a pattern of facial malformations and mental and physical growth impairments. But it is only recently that more moderate, social drinking has been shown to be potentially harmful, too.

Recent studies indicate that an average of one to two drinks daily can lead to decreased birth weight, growth abnormalities, and behavioral problems. Even lower levels of alcohol consumption don't seem to be safe. As few as one to two drinks twice weekly seem to increase the risk of spontaneous abortion as well as learning impairments. No safe minimum level of daily or weekly drinking during pregnancy has been established, which is why the U.S. Surgeon General has advised that "women avoid all alcoholic beverages during pregnancy because of their risk of birth defects."

Does that mean you should, in good conscience, not have a single drink throughout your entire pregnancy? It depends. The answer is yes, if you've battled to get off the bottle and doubt your ability to stop at one. However, most doctors believe a very occasional, celebratory drink (a champagne on your birthday, a beer at the annual company picnic) is harmless. The key is to make abstinence the norm, having a drink the rare exception.

Prescription and over-the-counter drugs. The general rule during pregnancy: never take any drugs, either prescription or non-prescription (including everyday items like aspirin, cough medicine, etc.), without consulting your doctor first. While some medications may be taken safely, other medicines can complicate pregnancy and/or cause birth defects, so it's always best to discuss a drug's safety with your doctor before using it.

Illicit drugs. The spectrum of ill effects that a fetus can suffer from exposure to recreational or illicit drugs is wide and ominous. Cocaine- or crack-exposed babies, for example, tend to have smaller-than-normal heads and brains, stiff limbs, extremely fragile nervous systems, besides facing an increased risk of missing a small intestine, having deformed genital and urinary tracts, and suffering from stroke, crib death, and seizure. Other habit-forming drugs, such as barbiturates, amphetamines, heroin, and methadone have been linked to low birth weight and behavioral disorders, and may force a newborn to suffer the effects of withdrawal after birth. Even marijuana and hashish smoking are unlikely to prove safer than the hard stuff. Research in animals has linked high doses of both to birth defects, although, to date, there have been no conclusive studies in humans.

There's no evidence that any of these illicit drugs are safe even in small doses. Preliminary evidence indicates that even a single cocaine or crack hit during pregnancy, for example, may cause some lasting damage. But the hopeful news is that if you quit drugs entirely now, you may be able to counter some of the ill effects if you stay in top shape nutritionally and otherwise for the rest of your pregnancy. Even if you have a drug habit, you can significantly reduce the risks to your baby-to-be by establishing an open, honest relationship with a doctor and working closely with him or her.

Parasites. Eating raw meat or coming in contact with cat feces containing the organism *Toxoplasma gondii* can give you an infection called toxoplasmosis. This infection may not cause any symptoms in you (if it does cause symptoms, they are mild and passing, similar to a slight flu), but can blind the fetus or damage its central nervous system. It's estimated that one to two babies per one thousand are born infected by toxoplasmosis.

If you've been exposed to the parasite prior to pregnancy, as about 35 percent of the U.S. population has, your baby is out of danger, since your body will have developed antibodies against reinfection. A simple blood test can determine whether you're immune or not.

If the blood test indicates that you've never met up with the parasite before, you'll need to take some precautions. All previously unexposed women need to be on guard for two things: 1. Since uncooked or poorly cooked meat can carry the parasite, you need to cook all meat and fowl to "well done" (140° F). Also, thoroughly wash hands, cutting boards, utensils, etc., after handling raw meat and poultry. 2. You should avoid areas (especially sandboxes) where cats may have defecated; if you do garden, be sure to wear gloves and wash your hands thoroughly afterward.

In addition, cat owners should ask someone else to change the kitty litter daily. Plus, the empty litter pan should be disinfected with a mixture of boiling water and bleach, then allowed to stand for five minutes, at least once a week. (If you must do the job yourself, wear disposable gloves and wash your hands immediately afterward.) Also, feeding your cat only well-cooked meat or commercial cat food lowers the chances that your cat will acquire the organism, as will keeping your cat indoors and not allowing it to hunt mice and birds.

In the rare event that a blood test reveals you have an active infection, your doctor will, in all likelihood, suggest you have the baby tested using a technique called percutaneous fetal blood sampling (PUBS). If the fetus is infected, many women opt to terminate the pregnancy since the consequences of the infection can be so severe. Drug therapy, however, is an option that seems capable of drastically limiting defect risks. The drug used in this country to treat toxoplasmosis, pyrimethamine, however, is not without risks to the fetus itself. A less toxic agent, and so far a seemingly safer one, is spiramycin, which is used widely in Europe and may be obtained in some cases in this country with special permission from the Food and Drug Administration. In addition, newborns exposed to the organism in the womb are usually treated with drugs after birth, too, to head off the possibility that complications such as hearing loss or retardation may arise in later years.

Electric blankets and electric clocks (placed at bedside). There is growing evidence that chronic exposure to low-level electromagnetic emissions (such as you get from these appliances) may increase the risk of birth defects, miscarriage, and other health problems. You may also be hazardously exposed to low-

❧   REVERSING RISKS YOU MAY ALREADY HAVE RUN   ❧

It's not unusual to worry about something that you ate, drank, or did before you realized you were pregnant. For weeks I worried that the Advil I had taken before I knew I was pregnant might have harmed the baby in some way. When I finally discussed my fear with my ob/gyn I realized the only mistake I had made was not talking with her sooner, since she reassured me that there was absolutely no reason for concern.

In the majority of cases, you'll be, like I was, relieved to discover you have little cause for worry. There are two reasons why: 1. The exposure you're worried about, was, in all likelihood, limited. Although it's safest to shield the fetus from potential toxic substances whenever possible, briefly exposing it to a hazard like cigarette smoke, alcohol, paint fumes, or hair dye before you realized you were pregnant is unlikely to cause permanent damage. 2. The fetus seems to have some ability to recover. There's evidence to suggest that good health habits throughout the rest of your pregnancy can help undo any damage low-level exposure to a hazard may have caused. The fetus, in other words, seems to be able to mend itself to some extent.

Perhaps the best way to find out about any risk you may have run before realizing you were pregnant is to talk with your doctor. There are also two paperbacks that extensively list pregnancy-risk information for brand-name drugs: *Peace of Mind during Pregnancy: An A–Z Guide to the Substances That Could Affect Your Unborn Baby*, by Christine Kelly-Bouchanan; (New York: Dell, 1989) and *Will It Hurt the Baby: The Safety of Medications during Pregnancy and Breastfeeding*, by Richard S. Abrams, M.D. (New York: Addison Wesley, 1990). It can't be denied that some substances do cause real harm (the acne medication Accutane, for instance, causes serious birth defects in an estimated 25 percent of exposed babies). But it also helps to remember that in the majority of cases your fears are worse than the facts.

level electromagnetic emissions (which are a form of radiation) when you work in front of a computer video display terminal (VDT) for several hours daily. However, the health risk is thought to be minimized if you work at the screen less than twenty hours a week, and/or sit twenty-eight inches from the screen and four feet from the sides and backs of other terminals (for more on work-related hazards, see pp. 60–63).

Household fumes. Benzene, turpentine, spray paints which contain M-butyl ketone (MBK), and other liquid paint removers have all been associated with birth defects. In addition, scraping off old paint (which may be lead-based) or tearing down old walls during a renovation could expose you to high concentrations of lead dust. (Note: although latex paints presently on the market are lead-free, about 10 or 20 percent of these paints still contain mercury, which has recently been associated with neurological damage. The safest course is to either avoid using all paints entirely during your pregnancy or telephone the paint manufacturer to find out if the product you want to use contains mercury. Mercury-free paints don't seem to pose any special danger.)

What about the wide array of other household products—ant and roach sprays, outdoor insecticides, weed killers, oven cleaners, flea and tick formulas, etc.—that contain potent chemicals? The effects of exposure to most of these products isn't fully known at this time; it's suspected, though, that only prolonged and repeated use is likely to pose a serious threat.

To be on the safe side, most experts recommend that you steer clear of using these products completely during your first trimester, when the embryo is in its most rapid stage of development. Afterward, if you must use a chemical-containing product, you should make sure to wear gloves, work in a well-ventilated area so the fumes can quickly and easily dispel, and avoid aerosol sprays (opt for pump sprays, which emit fewer toxic fumes, instead). Also, you may want to check your local health-food store for safer alternatives to both traditional housecleaning products and insect repellents.

IF YOU'RE CONSIDERING A VBAC

If you are thinking about attempting a vaginal birth after having had a cesarean section (VBAC), your choice of doctor is particularly important. "If your doctor is grudging or uneasy about a VBAC or feels it is dangerous, it is quite likely that even a slight variation in your labor pattern will cause him or her to recommend a repeat cesarean. On the other hand, many physicians believe in the safety and wisdom of VBACs and have a lot of confidence, experience and expertise. It is worth changing doctors to get one who will help you. And the best way to find the right doctor is to ask around; ask midwives or childbirth educators; ask at hospitals; ask friends; attend childbirth conferences or workshops in your area." So write authors Marianne Brorop Weston, Penny Simkin, and Kathy Keolker in the pamphlet "Vaginal Birth after Cesarean." This excellent pamphlet, which discusses the benefits and risks of a VBAC, provides advice on how to improve your chances for one, and looks at the emotional hurdles involved in trying for a VBAC, is "must" reading for anyone considering vaginal birth after a previous cesarean. It can be ordered for $.50 from Pennypress Inc., 1100 23rd Avenue East, Seattle, WA 98112; 206-325-1419.

3

MONTH TWO

(4½ TO 9 WEEKS)

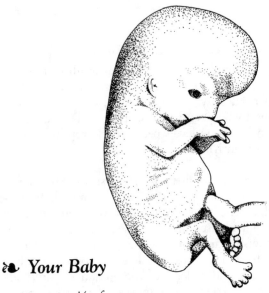

❧ *Your Baby*

WEIGHT: ⅓ of an ounce
LENGTH: 1 to 2 inches

Dramatic changes take place in the embryo's appearance this month. Unlike the first month, in which internal organs experience the most growth, during the second the external organs mostly take shape.

Flipperlike limbs mature into legs and arms with clearly defined ankles, knees, wrists, and elbows. Short stubby buds blossom into feet and hands with distinct toes and fingers. And where there was once a tiny tail, by the end of the ninth week there are tiny buttocks.

A face forms by month's end, too. Ears, eyes, eyelids, cheeks, nose, lips, and tongue all become recognizable. Because the embryo looks so unmistakably human at the end of the second month, it's renamed a fetus. However, body proportions are still somewhat askew. The fetal head is almost twice as large as its body because the brain grows at a much faster pace than the other internal organs. And the liver is larger than other organs, which makes the fetus appear to have a potbelly.

ᴥ *Your Body*

COMMON SIDE EFFECTS OF EARLY PREGNANCY

Some women hardly notice any body changes at all in the first trimester, while others begin to "feel" pregnant even before they've missed a period. So you may or may not experience the following symptoms (which tend to disappear or become more moderate as certain hormone levels peak, then drop, usually by the end of the third month).

Breast tenderness. During the first trimester a surge of hormones stimulates your breasts to enlarge and to prepare for milk production. Not only does the sheer volume of your breast tissue increase, making your breasts fuller and heavier, but your nipples, areolas (pigmented area around the nipples), and Montgomery tubercles (the little bumps or milk glands on the areolas) also tend to get darker and wider. All these changes can make your breasts and nipples feel quite sensitive and sore. Some women also experience a tingling, throbbing, or "congested" sensation.

By the end of the third to fourth month, your breasts are fully "prepped" for nursing. They stop growing at such a fast pace, and breast tenderness usually starts to subside. Until that happens, a good supportive bra can help alleviate the achiness caused by simple movement; if your nipples feel raw and hypersensitive, you can sometimes cut down on irritation by placing cotton balls or other soft material in your bra cups.

Fatigue. Feeling weary, drained, and exhausted is not unusual during the first trimester. Most women start to feel far more energetic once they are past the fourteenth week, again, probably, because hormone levels "settle down" by then. The only remedy for this tiredness is to give in to it whenever possible (take naps, slow down, go to bed earlier, etc.). Sometimes knowing that your exhaustion is a legitimate, physical pregnancy side effect, not a matter of mental ennui, laziness, or depression, can make giving in to it easier.

Lightheadedness and headaches. During early pregnancy, your expanding uterus and the myriad developments taking place in it need a generous flow of oxygen-rich blood. This high demand often results in a slightly lowered supply of oxygen-carrying blood to your brain—a deficit that can make you feel dizzy, faint, or, in some cases, give you a dull, throbbing headache. The best relief for these discomforts is rest: lying down will tend to cure all of them, including a headache. Dizzy spells and feelings of faintness can also be overcome, at least temporarily, by sitting for a few minutes with your head down between your knees, a position which sends pools of blood to your brain.

Increased saliva flow. Why some women experience an excess of mouth watering during early pregnancy is unknown, although the hormone progesterone is probably somehow to blame. Unfortunately, there is no real treatment for the condition, only the comfort of knowing that the saliva should stop flowing so copiously after the third month.

Numb or tingly limbs (Carpal tunnel syndrome). Some women feel unexplained pins-and-needles sensations in their wrists, hands, or arms (and sometimes legs) in the first trimester and/or throughout pregnancy. These sensations usually don't last for more than a few hours at a time and may be caused by the increased pressure put on nerves by the body's expanding fluid and blood volume.

Morning sickness. About half of all pregnant women experience morning sickness, a queasy feeling that can actually strike at any time of the day. Some women feel only mildly nauseated every once in a while; others can hardly keep a morsel down for weeks on end. Perhaps the only bright aspect of morning sickness is that it may be a positive sign of a healthy pregnancy, since some studies indicate that the risk of miscarriage is significantly lower when nausea or vomiting is present early in pregnancy.

There is no agreement as to what causes nausea during pregnancy. The rise of the hormone HCG (human chorionic gonadotropin) is frequently blamed, but there are also theories that blame low blood-sugar levels and a vitamin B-6 deficiency.

There aren't any remedies proven to successfully combat morning sickness, either. Medication is almost never prescribed today, since those used in the past often led to birth defects. In cases of severe vomiting that persists for more than a day or two, the course of action is usually hospitalization and intravenous administration of fluids and nutrients. But the nausea most women experience doesn't usually demand such drastic measures.

Despite the fact that there are no certain cures for morning sickness, there is no end to the recommendations purported to offer relief. The dietary advice given below is based on an effort to keep blood-sugar levels even. They're worth a try, although none are guaranteed to work.

• Eat dry crackers or toast before getting out of bed in the morning, then every two hours during the day.

• Drink beverages between meals (not with) and only very hot or cold ones; bouillon, tea, ginger ale, and apple and grape juice are best.

• Hard-boiled eggs and potatoes seem to be two foods that are particularly easy to digest.

• Eat a lot of little meals during the day rather than two or three big ones.

• Try to eat even if you don't feel hungry, since nausea can be even worse if your stomach is empty.

• Avoid fast, fried, fatty, greasy, rich, and spicy foods. Stick to plain, bland ones, like broiled chicken, bananas, rice, yogurt, cereal, applesauce, pasta, etc.

• Prenatal vitamins containing iron often can aggravate an already irritated stomach and intestinal lining, so many doctors recommend you skip taking them until your morning sickness subsides. One hundred milligrams a day of vitamin B-6, however, is proven to be safe, and may help relieve your nausea.

What if you absolutely can't keep food down? Can your baby get enough nutrition for good health? There is some evidence that indicates that women who lose weight in the first trimester have a greater risk of having premature labor and/or a low-birth-weight baby. But that risk seems to be greatly reduced when you make a concerted effort to "catch up" after your morning sickness subsides (which is usually around the fourteenth week). Still, it's safest to attempt to gain steadily and to eat despite your morning sickness if at all possible. Also, if your vomiting becomes severe and persists for more than twenty-four hours, contact your doctor.

Frequent urination. By the fourth to sixth week, your enlarging uterus may already be putting pressure on your bladder, thereby reducing its capacity to hold liquid. The result is that you may need to relieve yourself far more frequently than usual. By the twelfth week, though, your uterus will have risen farther up into your abdomen, thus relieving the pressure on your bladder and the problem of frequent urination.

Despite the inconvenience of having to make so many trips to the bathroom, it's important not to attempt to cure the problem by drinking fewer liquids. If anything, your body needs extra fluids now, both to keep your digestive system running smoothly and to provide your expanding blood supply with necessary fluids.

❧ Your Doctor Appointment

During your first obstetrical visit, your doctor will want to review your medical history to find out if you have any health problems that might affect the course and outcome of your pregnancy. This first visit usually also includes a pelvic examination, various laboratory tests, as well as a calculation of your due date.

HOW YOUR MEDICAL HISTORY MIGHT AFFECT
YOUR PREGNANCY

The following health conditions could demand special considerations during pregnancy.

Diabetes. If you are an insulin-dependent (Type I) diabetic, your chances of having a healthy baby are excellent if you control your blood sugar from the moment of conception (but preferably even before conceiving). Ninety percent of the babies born to diabetic women do *not* have birth defects and the majority of defects that do occur are minor, requiring little or no medical treatment and may not even be associated with the diabetes.

One of the keys to keeping your risks down is working closely with doctors who are experienced in diabetic pregnancies. The ideal treatment team, according to the American Diabetes Association, includes an internist interested in the treatment of diabetes, an obstetrician who is well versed in caring for pregnancies complicated by diabetes, and a pediatrician who has experience in treating newborns born to diabetic mothers. Your local affiliate of the ADA can help you find names of such doctors near you (the ADA should be listed in the white pages; if it's not, call 1-800-ADA-DISC or 1-703-549-1500 in the Virginia and metropolitan D.C. area for help). The ADA can also refer you to special literature, including its book, *Diabetes and Pregnancy: What to Expect,* and other information about diabetes in pregnancy.

Uterine fibroids. These benign, abnormal growths (which appear on the inside or outside of the uterus) usually don't cause any special problems. In rare cases, however, fibroids can become so large that they obstruct the opening of the uterus or block the cervix, making a vaginal delivery impossible. Although no special treatment of fibroids is usually required during pregnancy, to be on the safe side most doctors like to monitor fibroid growth carefully. That may involve more frequent-than-usual pelvic examinations and, possibly, periodic ultrasound examinations.

Chronic high blood pressure. When you have chronic high blood pressure, you have a higher than normal risk of having a baby who is premature and underweight. That's because high blood pressure can decrease the blood flow to the placenta, preventing the fetus from receiving adequate nourishment and oxygen. You also run a higher risk of developing preeclampsia, a dangerous high blood pressure condition that usually occurs after the twenty-eighth week (see pp. 101–03). But these risks can be lessened considerably when you keep your blood pressure carefully controlled throughout pregnancy.

Ideally, your blood pressure should be under control before you conceive. Once pregnant, your obstetrician may want to check your blood pressure two to three times a week. You also need to pay special attention to your diet, since it's believed that a diet that's deficient in protein contributes to the rising of blood-pressure levels.

If your blood pressure does begin to rise, you may receive strict advice to rest in bed, or, possibly, be required to stay in the hospital. But in general, if you follow your doctor's advice and eat well, your baby is unlikely to be adversely affected by your blood pressure problem.

Genital herpes and warts. If you have a history of herpes infections (you have had outbreaks before becoming pregnant), there's almost no chance—less than one in ten thousand according to some estimates—that your baby will be harmed. That's because you have already built up antibodies that prevent the virus from being passed on to your baby via the placenta. However, there is the possibility that you may need a cesarean delivery if you have active lesions at the time of delivery. When lesions are active, the baby could pick up the virus as he or she passes through the birth canal. A new lab test can accurately determine in just four hours whether your herpes infection is active (thus necessitating a c-section).

But genital herpes does pose a considerable danger to a fetus when a woman experiences her first outbreak during pregnancy. Almost 50 percent of babies born to mothers with a primary (first-time) infection give birth to babies who are also infected. Afflicted babies can suffer serious consequences, such as blindness, seizures, brain damage, and even death, because their immune systems can't fight off the virus.

Genital warts pose two risks during pregnancy. If warts are extensive and large, they can narrow or block the birth canal, making a cesarean delivery necessary. There is also the chance that you may transmit the infection to the fetus, who, years later, might develop warts on the larynx (which can be difficult to treat, but is not life-threatening). This risk appears to be slim, though. And since doctors aren't sure how the infection is passed on to a baby (if it's transmitted in utero, via the placenta, or contracted when passing through the birth canal), there is no consensus on whether a cesarean delivery provides protection when warts are present at the time of delivery.

Contraceptive use at the time of conception. Becoming pregnant when using spermicides or birth-control pills is not something you need to be especially concerned about. There's a clear scientific consensus that spermicide use at the time of conception is not associated with an increased risk of birth defects; if birth-control pills pose a risk (and many studies indicate they don't), then the risk appears to be a 2- to 3-percent increase in the chance of an early miscarriage.

The IUD isn't linked to an increased risk of birth defects, but having an IUD in place when you become pregnant does increase the chances of a first-trimester miscarriage. However, the IUD usually isn't removed (since removal itself can increase the odds of a spontaneous abortion).

Previous high-risk pregnancies. If you've experienced difficulties during previous pregnancies, you have a better-than-average chance of running into the same troubles again. On the positive side, at least this time you and your doctor are forewarned and so can take every possible precaution to detect, head off, and/or minimize complications in advance.

Your age. Being over thirty-five no longer instantly puts your pregnancy in the "high-risk" category. But some health problems are indisputably more common in expectant mothers who are in their late thirties and forties. Your doctor, for instance, is likely to be more concerned about the possibility of birth defects, since age can significantly increase the odds of them (see pp. 71–72). Women over thirty-five also have a greater chance of experiencing miscarriage, and of having certain health problems—like diabetes, fibroids, and high blood pressure—that can complicate pregnancy. But by and large, being an "older" mother-to-be doesn't require different care than that given to a younger woman.

Lab Tests

Besides checking your blood pressure and weight at every appointment, your doctor will also check your urine for a) signs of bacteria or urinary tract infection, which if left untreated can cause premature birth, and b) glucose or protein spillage, which can be signs of, respectively, gestational diabetes (see pp. 117–19) or pregnancy-induced high blood pressure (see pp. 101–03). Only on the initial visit, though, will your doctor need to draw blood samples to screen for the following diseases:

Syphilis and hepatitis B. These diseases can be seriously damaging to a baby if not detected and treated early in a pregnancy.

Rubella. The point is to make sure you're immune (most adults are) since this disease can produce severe birth defects. If you're not immune, your doctor will advise you on how to take special care to avoid contact with anyone who might have this disease.

Toxoplasmosis. Your immunity is checked (see pp. 38–39 for full discussion of the dangers of toxoplasmosis).

Anemia. This is a condition in which you are unable to produce enough red blood cells to properly fuel the transfer of oxygen to the fetus. Taking iron and/or folic acid supplements is usually all it takes to rectify this problem.

On your first prenatal visit, your doctor will draw a blood sample to determine whether you have the Rh factor, which is a type of protein you inherit on red blood cells. If you don't have it (about 15 percent of the population doesn't), you are considered Rh-negative. Being Rh-negative doesn't affect your general health at all, but unless you receive a special vaccine during pregnancy, it can potentially cause severe birth defects in your fetus.

When your blood is Rh-negative and your partner's is Rh-positive, there is a chance your unborn baby will inherit the Rh-positive factor. That's dangerous, because if your blood mixes with your baby's, you'll become Rh-sensitized, which means your body will begin producing antibodies to the Rh factor. These antibodies perceive Rh-positive fetal blood cells as harmful substances and so seek to destroy them.

If your partner is also Rh-negative, there is no risk of Rh-sensitization.

In a first pregnancy, the danger to the fetus is slight, since Rh-sensitization usually doesn't occur until after birth (maternal and fetal blood almost always meet and mix when the placenta is delivered). But if Rh antibodies are produced after a first delivery, the next Rh-positive pregnancy will be at high risk for problems. These problems can range from mild to severe. Babies born with mild cases of Rh disease may only require phototherapy for jaundice and a blood transfusion after birth; babies with severe Rh disease may suffer from brain damage, heart failure, or even death. (A new technique used during pregnancy—cordocentesis—in which blood is transfused to the fetus in utero via the umbilical cord, is helping to reduce the risks of severe Rh disease.)

Fortunately, Rh-sensitization is easy to prevent. A vaccine—Rho (D) immunoglobulin (Rhlg)—can stop your body from producing antibodies to Rh-positive cells. To be effective, the vaccine must be administered at twenty-eight weeks gestation and seventy-two hours after your first birth (or first miscarriage, ectopic pregnancy, or abortion). Rhlg should also be given after chorionic villi sampling and amniocentesis and must be given during each new pregnancy.

This lifesaving vaccine is given via injection. The only side effects you might experience are a slight fever and soreness at the injection site.

❧ Your Diet

GAINING THE RIGHT AMOUNT OF WEIGHT

Less than twenty years ago, most doctors told their patients to gain no more than fifteen to twenty pounds, and warned ominously that "any extra weight gained in pregnancy is likely to stay with you for the rest of your life." Today, weight-gain recommendations are much higher for several reasons. First, it's now known that gaining more weight leads to the birth of bigger babies. And full-term babies who weigh five and a half pounds or more tend to experience fewer illnesses, fewer disabilities, and have higher intelligence scores than lower birth-weight babies.

The higher weight-gain goals also reflect reality, since the majority of women gain a lot more than fifteen pounds. And because, compared to twenty years ago, women today are more likely to breast-feed (which helps melt off postpartum pounds) and know more about good diet and exercise habits, postpartum weight loss is less likely to be a problem.

Another change that has occurred over the years is that more experts realize that standard, blanket prescriptions for weight gain during pregnancy don't make sense. Instead, it's thought that weight-gain goals should be individualized, more tailored to a woman's build and whether she is thin or overweight prepregnancy. The chart on p. 55 incorporates these considerations and so should give you a realistic idea of the range of pounds you should (and probably will naturally) gain. It's adapted from *Nutrition for Your Pregnancy* by Judith E. Brown (University of Minnesota Press, 1983, Minneapolis).

The pace of your gain. Ideally you should gain your weight steadily, putting on three to eight pounds in the first trimester, then between three quarters and one pound every week thereafter.

Some women, though, experience such severe morning sickness that they actually lose weight in the first months. Although the rate of premature birth is higher for women who don't gain weight in the initial months of pregnancy, the risk appears to be significantly reduced if, after a poor start, you "catch up" and achieve your recommended total weight gain by the end of pregnancy.

For women who gain too much too soon, the recommendation is *don't diet*. Dieting prevents you from providing the fetus with adequate nutrients and can lead to fetal growth retardation. Instead of dieting, you should try to moderate your weight gain to one pound a week by cutting out sweets and fatty foods.

Weight worries. Most women monitor their pregnancy weight gain with some anxiety—to put it mildly. I know that I worried that I was gaining too much while my sister was concerned that she was gaining too little. Although you probably won't be able to become indifferent to what the scale says, you may be able to diffuse some uneasiness by discussing your weight with your doctor. After each weigh-in, simply ask, "Am I gaining at a healthy rate?"

If you're concerned about gaining, you may be reassured if you know how the weight divides up and how you can expect it to be lost afterward. If you gain thirty-one pounds, for example, here's how the weight will be distributed:

Breast enlargement	3 pounds
Blood volume increase	5 pounds
Maternal fat and protein stores	8 pounds
Placenta	2 pounds
Amniotic fluid	3 pounds
Baby	8 pounds
Uterus weight gain	2 pounds
Total Weight Gain	31 pounds

At the moment of delivery, you lose approximately thirteen to fifteen pounds (the average weight of the baby, amniotic fluid, and placenta combined). If you breast-feed (which burns almost five hundred calories a day), you'll tend to lose about one half to one pound a week until you reach your prepregnancy weight (usually somewhere between six weeks and three months postpartum). If you don't breast-feed, your weight loss will tend to be a little less rapid. Shaking the last five to ten pounds may also take a little more conscious effort.

RECOMMENDED WEIGHT GOALS DURING PREGNANCY
Pre-Pregnancy Weight

Height without Shoes	Underweight If You Weighed This or Less	Normal Weight Range*	Overweight If You Weighed This or More
4'10"	88	89–108	109
4'11"	91	92–112	113
5'	94	95–115	116
5'1"	99	100–121	122
5'2"	104	105–127	128
5'3"	108	109–132	133
5'4"	113	114–138	139
5'5"	118	119–144	145
5'6"	123	124–150	151
5'7"	127	128–155	156
5'8"	132	133–161	162
5'9"	137	138–167	168
5'10"	142	143–173	174
5'11"	146	147–178	179
6'	151	152–184	185
YOUR RECOMMENDED GAIN GOAL FOR PREGNANCY	28–36 lbs Underweight	24–32 lbs Normal Weight	20–24 lbs Overweight

*Normal weight, "thin-boned" women will be closer to the lower end of this range; "big-boned" women will be closer to the higher end.

ৰ   *MAIL-ORDER MATERNITY WEAR*   ৰ

Even if you have never bought clothes through the mail before, being pregnant may prompt you to try it, since the maternity fashions available in stores are often so limited. All the catalogs listed below can be ordered free.

Motherhood Catalog
P.O. Box 2142
Santa Monica, CA 90406-2142
800-227-1903

MothersWork Maternity
52 West 57th Street
2nd Floor
New York, NY 10019
212-399-9840

ReCreations
P.O. Box 091038
Columbus, OH 43209
800-621-2547

Garnet Hill
262 Main Street
Franconia, NH 03580
800-622-6216
Primarily a catalog of natural fiber sheets, blankets, etc., but includes a few maternity and baby items

Motherwear
Box 114
Northampton, MA 01061
413-586-3488
Primarily a catalog of fashions for breast-feeding

Hanna Anderson
1010 NW Flanders Street
Portland, OR 97209
800-222-0544
A catalog of children's clothing that includes some maternity clothes

❧ *Your Workout*

THE VIGOROUS EXERCISE DEBATE

If you have entered pregnancy in top condition, the American College of Obstetricians and Gynecologists (ACOG) exercise guidelines (detailed on pp. 30–31) may seem restrictive to you. Is it possible to exceed the ACOG rules without harming the fetus? As yet, there's no clear-cut answer.

Some doctors, for instance, feel that if you've gone into pregnancy highly fit there is no reason not to continue exercising at the same level; as proof, they cite various case studies in which exercise was found to have no adverse effect upon athletes who exercised throughout their pregnancies or their babies.

Yet other obstetricians remain wary. Their major concerns are:

Oxygen supply. A recent study found that as pregnant women recovered from heavy exercise, the fetus's heartbeat slowed. This decrease in heartbeat could mean that after a vigorous workout, oxygen-carrying blood is diverted to your muscles and skin and away from your uterus. That, in turn, might mean that your baby is being deprived of oxygen for a short time. Despite this finding, however, it should be noted that none of the women or their babies involved in the study seemed to suffer any ill effects that could be linked to exercising.

Body temperature. Any time your temperature goes up, as it often does with strenuous exercise, the fetus's goes up also. But there's a difference: unlike you, who can sweat, the fetus has no way to get rid of excess heat. The fear here is that the fetus might overheat and thus injure its central nervous system. Although there is no evidence that this has ever happened in humans, studies done on pregnant animals have shown an association between exercise, body temperature increases, and nervous-system defects. Critics of these studies note that the animals used were untrained and driven to exhaustion.

Birth weight. Babies born to women who exercise heavily tend to be lighter in weight at birth than the babies of women who exercise less or not at all, according to at least one study. What the significance of this is, though, is far from clear, since the babies born to women who exercised vigorously were not classified "underweight." In fact, they were lively, energetic, and thriving at birth.

Joint laxity. During pregnancy, hormones cause the bands of tissue that connect joints to slacken and soften. The worry is that this might make you more vulnerable to pulls, tears, and dislocations. How warranted this worry is—whether this softening does indeed make you more injury-prone—has not been studied.

Clearly, many of the fears about heavy exercise during pregnancy are far from substantiated. Still, even obstetricians who are "pro vigorous exercise" stress these points:

• If you want to go beyond the ACOG guidelines for moderate aerobic exercise, you should get your doctor's approval first. Plus, you should work closely with your physician to make sure your workouts aren't having any detrimental effect on you or your baby.

• High-level workouts should only be pursued by pregnant women in top-notch condition. In other words, you shouldn't try to *increase* your level of training during pregnancy, only continue what you were doing before conceiving.

• Be open and attuned to the possibility that you may have different limits when pregnant; you may simply be too tired at times to do what came easily before you became pregnant. According to many obstetricians, the key to exercising safely during pregnancy is to be flexible and not push yourself too much. Simply, you must learn to quit if you're feeling worn out or if an exercise feels uncomfortable, and accept the fact that if you don't feel better after a workout, it's probably a sign you are overexerting yourself.

❧ *Your Feelings*

SEX DURING PREGNANCY

The one generalization that can be made about sex during pregnancy is that you can expect it to be different from sex prior to conception.

For some women, some of the time, sex is significantly better: they find they have enormous vitality and a lively interest in sex. Besides feeling sensual and spontaneous, they find enjoyment is enhanced by the physical changes that pregnancy sparks. The increase in blood flow, for instance, can make the genital area in some women more arousable and sensitive, even causing some women to experience multiple orgasms for the first time. The increase in the production of vaginal secretions may make lubrication and wetness easier for some, while many women find that as their breasts get larger, they become more responsive to stimulation.

Yet these same physical changes hinder pleasure for other women. They find the increase in blood flow uncomfortably congests the tissue around the outer portion of the vagina, making penetration difficult and "cooling down" after lovemaking uncomfortable (since the increased blood flow can cause the genitals to stay swollen and engorged for up to an hour afterward). More profuse vaginal secretions may make oral sex less desirable for some couples; some women find that their enlarged breasts become too tender for fondling.

Obviously, if you spend your first trimester feeling exhausted and nauseated, you'll be feeling less desirous. And it's not uncommon to feel too awkward, uncomfortable, and preoccupied in the third trimester to enjoy sex with great frequency.

Men react differently to sex during pregnancy, too. Some find the pregnant body a terrific turn-on; they bask in their partner's ballooning belly, softening skin, enlarging breasts. Yet others discover the presence of a kicking, moving fetus a hindrance to arousal. They find it difficult to feel sexually charged and "fatherly" at the same time. Many men, despite information to the contrary, can't overcome their fear that penetration may harm the fetus somehow.

Given that there are no hard-and-fast rules as to how you and your partner will feel at various stages, perhaps the best perspective to have about sex during pregnancy is to not have inflexible expectations (don't worry, for instance, if you make love less frequently than before). Also, it helps to be sensitive to each other's changing states of mind, to accept ebbs and flows in desire as normal, and to be as open as possible to discussing each other's needs, worries, and desires.

When sex may not be safe. Most doctors feel that if you have a history of miscarriages, bleeding, pain, or premature labor, if your partner is at risk for having a sexually transmitted disease, or, in some cases, if you are carrying more than one fetus, sex may not be safe during pregnancy. But insist that your doctor give you a full explanation of what abstinence means, since in some cases it simply means no overly "vigorous" lovemaking.

If your pregnancy is uneventful, though, there's a consensus among doctors that making love is safe up until at least the last six weeks. But there are two practices that should be avoided throughout: vaginal after anal penetration, which can cause serious infection, and blowing air into the vagina, which may cause an air embolism (a pocket of air in the bloodstream that can cause a possibly fatal stroke).

After the eighth month, there's little agreement among doctors whether intercourse (and orgasm) is safe. Some doctors fear that sex may trigger premature labor; they also worry that the penis could introduce bacteria just as the cervix begins to open or as your membranes rupture. Other experts feel confident that sex is safe right through to labor. Given these conflicting views (and the lack of definitive research data), most couples find they follow their instincts about what feels right and comfortable.

❧ Your Life-Style

WORK-RELATED HAZARDS

Many working women worry about the possible effects their job may have on their unborn baby. These concerns are not frivolous given the growing number of work-related activities and job environments that are now being linked to an increased risk of miscarriage, preterm birth, and birth defects.

When the work dangers are clear-cut (when, for example, your job exposes you to toxic chemicals proven to cause birth defects), there are medical guidelines and laws to ensure that you are transferred to a position that's safe for your fetus and that offers comparable pay. But there are still thousands of professions that *may* pose a health threat to a developing baby, but, because the medical evidence is still murky, no one has yet established guidelines or laws dictating how or whether your employer must protect you.

What if, for example, your work requires you to stay long hours (over twenty per week) before a video display terminal (VDT)? This is a situation that chronically exposes you to low-level electromagnetic emissions (which are a form of radiation) and which recent preliminary reports have linked to an increased risk of miscarriage. But there is still no conclusive medical data (as well as considerable controversy) about what the health risks really are. So what do you do? Your first recourse might be to try to persuade your employer to let you do other types of work and/ or cut down your hours at the VDT (the miscarriage risk is believed to be lessened if you work under twenty hours a week at a VDT and sit twenty-eight inches away from your screen and at least forty-eight inches away from the sides and backs of other terminals). More and more large companies, in particular, are willing to make these kinds of compromises, partly out of fear of legal liability.

If your employer refuses your request, you might ask your union (if you belong to one) to intervene in your behalf. You may also have some legal ammunition through the Federal Pregnancy Discrimination Act, which requires that pregnant employees get the same benefits as employees who cannot work due to other illnesses or injuries. For example, if your employer offers paid or unpaid sick leave, your pregnancy would make you eligible for it as long as your doctor supports your reasons for requesting it. In addition, many states now have laws or rules on pregnancy leave and related issues; you may also qualify for state unemployment or temporary disability benefits.

Birth-defect hotlines. To get up-to-date scientific data on whether your particular job poses any risk, there are two hotlines you can call: the Pregnancy Environment Hotline, at 617-787-4957; or the Science Information Division of the March of Dimes, at 914-428-7100. There are also two resources your doctor can tap for you: the Teratogen Information System at the University of Texas Health Science Center in Dallas, and the Reproductive Toxicology Center in Washington, D.C. Both pro-vide, exclusively to doctors, the latest data on chemicals, drugs, food additives, environments, etc., that might have birth-defect potential.

In addition, studies have linked the jobs listed on p. 63 to an increased risk for birth defects and/or premature birth. If you work in any of these occupations, you should discuss the risks with your doctor. Do try, however, not to become overly alarmed. Not only is the data still inconclusive in most cases, but your exposure at this stage of pregnancy is likely to have been limited enough not to have greatly increased the risk of complications.

ঽ&   *AN ALERT FOR WOMEN WHO WORK/LIVE*   ঽ&
                  WITH YOUNG CHILDREN

Mini-epidemics of any number of viruses tend to sweep through day-care centers, kindergartens, and elementary schools, affecting whole classrooms of children. For the most part, these viruses cause minor symptoms (runny nose, fever, rash, etc.) in the children and adults who contract them. But when a pregnant woman is exposed to some of these viruses, her fetus may be put at serious risk for birth defects. That's why any woman who works in a day-care center, a school cafeteria, or is a mother or teacher of school-age children needs to take precautions. First of all, if there is a virus "going around," you should contact your doctor: find out if the particular virus poses a risk to your fetus and if there is a blood test to check for your susceptibility. If you are not immune, you may then need to avoid contact with anyone likely to carry the infection until either your pregnancy is over or the virus ceases to circulate in your community. Also, any pregnant woman who works with children should wash her hands religiously, especially after wiping a runny nose or holding hands. And if your job involves changing diapers, you should wear plastic gloves, since some viruses can be passed along in urine.

JOB RISKS*

Occupation	Potential Hazard
Textile worker (sewer, stitcher, upholsterer)	Synthetic fiber dust, dyes, flame retardants, asbestos, formaldehyde
Hospital worker (nurse, aides, orderlies, dental hygienists, lab workers)	Anesthetic gases, X-ray radiation, infectious diseases, toxic chemicals, medicines
Electronics assemblers	Lead, tin, epoxy resins, toxic chemicals
Hairdressers and cosmetologists	Aerosol propellants, hair dyes, nail-polish solvents, acetone, hair-spray resins, ethyl alcohol
Launderers, dry cleaners	Soap, detergents, industrially contaminated clothing, solvents
Photographers and developers	Caustics, iron salts, bromides, and other chemicals and acids
Plastic fabricators	A wide variety of chemicals and solvents
Artists, ceramicists, potters, sign painters and letterers	Lead oxide, trace metals, pigments
Opticians and lens grinders	Dust solvents, hydrocarbons, iron oxide

*A job not on this list but deserving of mention is that of airplane crew member. Preliminary data suggests that the high levels of radiation from the sun that both pilots and flight attendants are exposed to may be dangerous to a developing fetus. Although this is still a theory—there's no hard proof at this point that radiation exposure from air travel has actually led to illness or birth defects—if you work on an airplane or if your job entails an unusual amount of flying at high altitudes, you may want to consider flying only at low altitudes (flights within the U.S. are usually low altitude, while flights to Europe and Asia tend to be at high altitudes), or consider taking a leave of absence during your pregnancy.
Source: J. B. Kotch, C. C. Ossler, and D. C. Howze, "A Policy Analysis of the Problem of the Reproductive Health of Women in the Workplace," *Journal of Health Policy* (June 1984): 213.

4

MONTH THREE
(9 TO 13½ WEEKS)

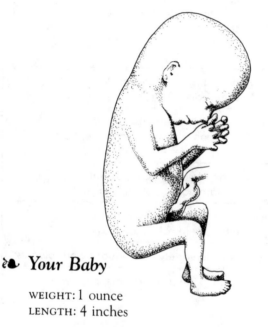

❧ *Your Baby*

WEIGHT: 1 ounce
LENGTH: 4 inches

Before this month, internal organs were primarily being formed. Now they actually start to function. The stomach and liver begin to produce digestive juices; the pancreas starts to manufacture insulin-producing cells; the gall bladder secretes bile; and rudimentary kidneys begin to process wastes (the fetus actually "pees" a little bit every day into the amniotic fluid).

The fetus's mouth and throat also become functional by month's end. It becomes capable of performing the two skills most crucial for survival outside the womb: sucking and swallowing.

Muscles twitch and are developed enough to be exercised. Although you can't feel the movements yet, the fetus is quite active, stretching and kicking almost constantly.

❧ *Your Body*

PREGNANCY LOSS

Early miscarriage. Thirty-one percent of all pregnancies end in miscarriage in the first three months. Yet few women are prepared for a pregnancy's end.

The symptoms of an impending miscarriage ("spontaneous abortion" in medical terms) are vaginal bleeding (the bleeding usually becomes increasingly heavy and begins to contain clots or tissue), low-back pain, feelings of no longer being pregnant (your breasts stop feeling full or tender, for instance), and/or abdominal cramping. These cramps can become quite painful and intense, akin in many ways to labor pains.

But it's important to remember that bleeding during pregnancy doesn't always result in miscarriage. If the bleeding is light, brownish, and there's no cramping, you may be experiencing what is known as "implantation bleeding." This usually occurs at about the same time you would have had your period and happens when the fertilized egg attaches itself to the wall of the uterus. No treatment is needed for this. The bleeding stops on its own in a day or two and then your pregnancy progresses as normal.

Reddish-brownish bleeding unaccompanied by pain may also be due to an inflammation or irritation of the cervix, which can be quite tender and easily bruised, especially after sex. This also poses no threat to the pregnancy and should stop by itself in a day or two.

Even if the blood is bright red, a miscarriage may still not be imminent if the bleeding is not accompanied by cramping. It's not well understood why this crampless bleeding occurs, although one guess is that it comes from the tissue lining the uterus, which seems, in some instances, to swell and shed quite extensively without any harm done to the developing embryo.

Whenever you experience bleeding during pregnancy, you should always contact your doctor. Doubtless, too, the first question you'll want an answer to is: will or won't my bleeding lead to a miscarriage? About 50 percent of the women who experience bleeding during pregnancy go on to deliver normal, healthy babies. And there are medical tests that can help predict what the outcome of your bleeding will be.

A pelvic examination can reveal if your cervix is opening, a sign that a miscarriage is likely. As early as six weeks into your pregnancy, an ultrasound examination can detect the fetus's heartbeat, the presence of which is an excellent sign that a miscarriage *won't* occur.

In some cases, neither a pelvic exam nor an ultrasound will provide a definitive answer as to whether a miscarriage is pending. Your doctor may then decide to order a series of at least two blood tests (done on different days) to detect your levels of HCG (human chorionic gonadotropin)—the hormone that maintains pregnancy. If your HCG levels are dropping (instead of doubling every two days as they should), it's an indication that the pregnancy is in trouble.

There may be a considerable amount of time and waiting between when you first suspect a problem and actually know if a miscarriage is likely. These hours (or days, sometimes even weeks) are likely to be filled with hope ("Maybe the bleeding will stop and the pregnancy be saved"), anger ("Why me?"), and feelings of being vulnerable and powerless. You may wonder:

• Can I do something to prevent this?

There are no known, proven measures to stop a miscarriage from happening once it's set in motion. Still, many doctors will advise you to rest (as well as to avoid sexual intercourse and tampon use). Whether bed rest does any good in preventing a threatened miscarriage isn't known, but it doesn't do any harm and you may welcome the advice to rest as you respond to the stress of this extremely difficult situation.

• Did I do something to cause this?

It's common to blame yourself when you think you may be miscarrying. But there is no evidence that emotional stress or physical exertion (such as jogging, dancing, or vigorous sex) is responsible for spontaneous abortion. Nor, in most cases, does a previous abortion make you more susceptible to miscarriage.

• Why does early miscarriage occur?
The chain of events that ends with a miscarriage seems to start with an abnormal division of chromosomes. This causes the egg to develop poorly; poor development leads to the death of the egg; the death of the egg causes a drop in hormones, which causes the egg to be expelled from the uterus. This series of events is not hereditary; in the vast majority of cases, miscarriage is a random occurrence that can't be prevented or controlled. Luckily, miscarriage is also an event that rarely occurs more than once or twice in a woman's lifetime.

Doctor's tend to view miscarriage as a natural, normal part of life. While a miscarriage may be a deeply emotional occurrence for you, an obstetrician/gynecologist's perspective is that it is a common, practically everyday event (since, remember, almost one out of every three pregnancies ends in miscarriage). That's why most doctors don't recommend any special testing after a single miscarriage. In general, it's only after the second or third miscarriage that most doctors will begin to hunt for a cause.

Recurrent miscarriage, which is defined as more than three consecutive miscarriages, can often be traced to a number of factors. Genetic flaws may cause consecutive losses; this problem is found in less than 1 percent of the population and can be confirmed via an expensive blood analysis called a karyotype. Some abnormalities of the uterus, such as a double uterus or fibroids, can prevent the fertilized egg from implanting properly. Certain infections, bacteria, and viruses, if left untreated, may cause repeated miscarriages. Insufficient production of the hormone progesterone has also been linked to miscarriage, although not all doctors agree that this is a factor. Finally, there's conjecture that there may be an immunologic cause why some women repeatedly miscarry. Some women, it's believed, may lack "blocking antibodies" that prevent the body from rejecting the fetus as a foreign invader. Experiments aimed at boosting a woman's immune system, with medications and/or the injection of white blood cells, are under way, but success rates are still unknown.

• What medical attention do I need? None, if your uterus expels its entire contents by itself. But if all tissue isn't passed (you keep bleeding), you'll need a D&C (dilatation and curettage), in which the uterus is gently cleaned of any fragments. These procedures usually require a few hours hospitalization and general anesthesia.

• When can I try to get pregnant again? When a miscarriage occurs early, within the first eight weeks, and is complete (does not require a D&C), studies indicate it's safe to try again right away, during the very next menstrual cycle. If, however, you miscarry after eight weeks and/or require a D&C, many doctors advise you to wait for two regular menstrual cycles before trying again.

• What are the prospects for my next pregnancy? Most miscarriages cast no reflection on your ability to conceive and to have a healthy pregnancy. Studies show that your odds of having a normal pregnancy after a single miscarriage are the same as for a woman who never lost a baby. Even after two losses the risk of it happening a third time is only 5 percent higher than for the general population.

• Is what I'm feeling normal? No two women respond identically to a miscarriage, but most experience a period of mourning, with some needing longer to grieve than others.

You may first react with shock: "I can't believe this happened to me." You may feel guilt, too, and find that you pick over everything that you "shouldn't" have done: "If only I hadn't gone skiing," "If only I hadn't jogged," "If only I hadn't had those terrible thoughts."

When my first pregnancy ended in miscarriage, I became preoccupied with finding something to blame. I analyzed everything I had done in hopes of uncovering the "act" that provoked the miscarriage. I also searched out every bit of scientific information I could find on miscarriage in the hope that I would gain more insight into its cause. It was extremely difficult for me to accept my miscarriage as a random, common event for which there really is no treatment.

You may also find it difficult to be around other women's babies after a miscarriage; you may feel vulnerable around the time the baby would have been born; you may feel nervous about having to face people and explain, "I am no longer pregnant." I know that I didn't stop worrying about whether I would ever be able to have a healthy pregnancy until I was several months along in my next pregnancy.

Realizing that your feelings and reactions are, to a large extent, universal may not relieve your sadness or anxiety, but it may help you to accept your emotions and worries as natural. It can also be reassuring to know that you are not alone; like countless other women who have suffered through the sadness of miscarriage, you are likely to go on to experience healthy, problem-free pregnancies.

Ectopic pregnancy. About 1 percent of all pregnancies are ectopic, meaning they don't embed normally in the uterus but implant and grow elsewhere, usually in a fallopian tube. The danger in this is that a fallopian tube cannot expand to accommodate a fast-growing embryo. If an ectopic pregnancy is not diagnosed and removed early, the tube can burst, causing severe bleeding within the abdomen. Emergency surgery for the removal of the entire tube is then usually necessary. But luckily this scenario is increasingly rare today, since the majority of ectopic pregnancies are being diagnosed and treated before a rupture occurs.

There are several factors that put you at greater risk for an ectopic pregnancy. Pelvic inflammatory disease (PID) can damage a tube, causing the egg to get "caught" inside instead of passing freely through it. Endometriosis can create adhesions on and around the tubes, thus pinching them together and interfering with easy passage of an egg. Becoming pregnant with an IUD in place, having undergone previous tubal surgery, and, possibly, having been exposed to DES (a synthetic estrogen some women took to prevent miscarriage between 1940 and 1972) in utero also increases the odds of ectopic pregnancy.

There are two symptoms characteristic of most ectopic pregnancies: sharp, sudden abdominal pain, and/or vaginal bleeding. Other symptoms include shoulder pain, weakness, dizziness, and/or faintness. If you feel any of these symptoms you should contact your doctor right away (although the odds are in your favor, 100:1, that your pregnancy is *not* ectopic).

To diagnose an ectopic pregnancy, a doctor will usually first perform a pelvic exam, in which signs of an abnormal mass can sometimes be detected. In addition, a series of blood tests may be ordered to detect HCG (human chorionic gonadotropin—the pregnancy-maintaining hormone) to see if your levels are below normal, and an ultrasound may be ordered, too, to help determine the location of the pregnancy.

To treat an ectopic pregnancy usually requires surgery, either a laparoscopy (which leaves you with a tiny, almost invisible scar in your belly button) or laparotomy, which requires a larger, three- to eight-inch abdominal incision. If the tube is unruptured, it may not need to be removed; in fact, the earlier an ectopic pregnancy is diagnosed, the greater the chances are that the embryo can be removed, with the fallopian tube left intact.

Discovering you have an ectopic pregnancy can evoke all the mixed feelings a miscarriage does. But in some ways it can even be more difficult, since the anxiety and fear of having surgery is an added element. You may also, naturally, be hyperconcerned about your future ability to have a normal pregnancy. But your chances of not having a second tubal pregnancy are good—about 88 percent.

Still, you'll need to have your next pregnancy closely monitored. If you experience another ectopic pregnancy, close monitoring will detect it early, thus ensuring your future fertility. Close monitoring can also help your doctor rule out the possibility of another ectopic pregnancy within a week or two after your first missed period, and the earlier you have that positive verdict, the sooner you'll have peace of mind about the pregnancy.

Late miscarriage. Late miscarriage is defined as one that occurs after fourteen but before twenty weeks. It is relatively rare compared to early miscarriage. The cause of late miscarriage is also easier to trace and treat. One cause is an "incompetent cervix," in which the muscle at the bottom of the uterus is too weak to support the weight of the developing fetus and enlarging uterus. When an incompetent cervix is the cause of a late miscarriage, there is no pain or cramps before the fetus is expelled. The next pregnancy can be protected by what is known as the cerclage procedure, in which the cervix is stitched closed, usually before the sixteenth week, to prevent the cervix from weakening and opening. Stitches stay in place until about thirty-seven weeks; labor and delivery can then begin normally and naturally.

Late miscarriage can also be caused by a variety of infections (such as rubella or a sexually transmitted disease) and systemic diseases (like uncontrolled diabetes, kidney disease, or lupus). An undiagnosed blood incompatibility between an Rh-negative mother and an Rh-positive fetus can also cause late miscarriage (see "Find Out Your Rh Factor," pp. 52–53).

Spotting, bleeding, and/or cramping may signal an impending miscarriage and so should be immediately reported to your doctor.

The feelings of shock, grief, yearning, anger, and depression that are common with an early miscarriage may be even more intense when a late miscarriage occurs (since by that time a woman may already have felt her baby move). In fact, a late miscarriage is often experienced not so much as an end to a pregnancy but as the death of a baby. Healing may be easier for some couples if they go through some of the rituals and actions that are recommended for couples who have experienced a stillbirth or infant loss (see "When a Newborn Dies," p. 230).

૨૦ *Your Doctor Appointment*

PRENATAL TESTING:
ARE YOU A CANDIDATE MEDICALLY?

Evaluating your risk. Your doctor determines whether you are—according to medical criteria—a candidate for prenatal testing. For instance, you may fit certain medical criteria that put you at high risk for having a child with birth defects, but for religious or moral reasons you decide you don't want to be tested. And vice versa: you may be at very low risk in a medical determination, yet still decide for emotional reasons you really want a prenatal diagnosis. Here, then, is a look at when testing is *medically* recommended (see pp. 79–81, for "The Psychological Side of Prenatal Testing").

If he or she hasn't already done so, this month your obstetrician will give you a questionnaire that's designed to determine your chances of bearing a child with a birth defect. You'll find most of the questions aim to find out if you fit into any of the following "high-risk" categories:

• Being thirty-five years old or older. Genetic testing is usually recommended for women over thirty-five years old, since the risk of giving birth to a child with a chromosomal abnormality increases dramatically at that age. For instance, at age thirty, the chances of having a Down's syndrome baby (one who is "mentally retarded") is 1 in 900; at thirty-five years, 1 in 385; at forty-one years, 1 in 85.

• Having a family history of genetic diseases. A couple with a close blood relative who has a child with birth defects, or who have had a child with birth defects themselves, are usually encouraged to consider prenatal testing. That's because certain conditions tend to "run in families," and once you've had a child with a defect, the risk of having another usually increases.

• Being a member of an at-risk ethnic/cultural group. Certain disorders are carried more commonly in the genes of certain groups: for example, sickle-cell anemia is a blood disease that chiefly affects blacks; Tay-Sachs disease is a fatal enzyme deficiency disorder that mainly affects Jews of Central and Eastern European ancestry; beta-thalassemia is a blood disorder that mostly strikes people of Mediterranean descent.

Genetic counseling. If your doctor feels you are at risk for having a child with birth defects or if you have already decided to undergo prenatal testing, he or she will usually refer you to a genetic counselor—a professional who has had special training in genetics. The counselor will want to meet with you and your partner to take a detailed family history, perhaps construct a family tree and, in some cases, recommend further laboratory testing. The counselor will then calculate and explain exactly what your risks for birth defects are; exactly what prenatal testing can and can't reveal; and what your options might be after a diagnosis. The counselor's role is to explain and to answer any questions you might have; the decision to undergo a test is entirely yours.

The Tests

The following five tests help determine if your fetus is likely to be suffering from the effects of a faulty gene and/or if he or she is growing at a healthy, normal rate. Some of the procedures can be performed in a doctor's office; others in a hospital. Even when you are referred to a hospital for testing, however, it's almost always on an outpatient basis.

Ultrasound

Timing: Anytime during pregnancy

Purpose: In early pregnancy: to find out the cause of bleeding or pain, to diagnose a miscarriage or ectopic pregnancy, to date the age of the fetus, to locate the placenta, to determine the number of fetuses. In mid-pregnancy: to identify any gross structural abnormalities, such as missing limbs, polycystic kidneys, anencephaly (incomplete formation of the brain), and hydrocephaly (water on the brain). The sex of the baby can usually be determined at this stage. In the last trimester: to locate the position of the baby, to assess the volume of amniotic fluid, and to tell whether a fetus is the appropriate size for its gestational age.

Procedure: Ultrasound bounces beams of sound waves off the uterus, catches the echoes, and then constructs a picture out of them. An ultrasound examination is painless, although some require you to have a full bladder and that can get uncomfortable. In abdominal ultrasound, a small transducer or microphone that has been covered with a translucent gel is moved across your belly and scans the fetus's and your organs. The pictures produced by these sound waves are visible to you and the ultrasound examiner on a small television-like screen. A vaginal ultrasound works the same way, except that the transducer is a small wand which is covered with a condom and then placed at the opening (not deep inside) your vagina. An ultrasound examination takes anywhere from five to thirty minutes to perform.

Results: May be available during actual procedure, if the ultrasound examiner is willing to tell you the results on the spot. Some examiners will only give results to your doctor, who will then discuss the findings with you afterward.

Accuracy: Able to detect anomalies with extreme accuracy in early and mid-pregnancy; in the last trimester, it may be less precise, especially in determining fetal age and/or weight because of the fetus's tight fit in the uterus, the mother's weight, and a variety of other factors.

Risks: So far, it has not been implicated in causing any harm to either you or the fetus. But ultrasound has only been in clinical use for fifteen years, so there is still the possibility (considered slight by experts) that there are unknown long-term side effects.

Amniocentesis

Timing: Fifteen to eighteen weeks (sometimes earlier or later)

Purpose: To detect chromosomal and developmental abnormalities

Procedure: It's done as you lie down on an examining table. A pre-amnio ultrasound determines the position of the fetus and placenta and whether there is enough amniotic fluid to sample. A slender needle is then inserted through the abdominal wall into the amniotic sac, where a small amount of fluid (one ounce) is extracted (sometimes a local anesthetic is first injected into the site of needle insertion). The fluid withdrawal only takes a few minutes—most women don't find it painful per se, but do find it "uncomfortable" since they feel the pressure of a needle in their abdomen.

Results: It takes three to four weeks to culture fetal cells from the amniotic fluid and analyze them.

Accuracy: Considered highly accurate

Risks: The risk of miscarriage is increased by about 1 percent. Complications, such as infection, bleeding, leaking of amniotic fluid, or fetal injury are extremely rare. But a recent preliminary study found that children whose mothers had amniocentesis seemed to experience more ear infections (infections treatable with antibiotics) during the first years of life than children of mothers who didn't have the test. Why this might be so, and whether other studies will bear out this finding, isn't yet known.

Chorionic Villi Sampling (CVS)

Timing: Nine to eleven weeks, although it is sometimes performed earlier or later.

Purpose: To detect chromosomal abnormalities or genetically inherited diseases.

Procedure: Involves removing a sample of placental tissue (chorionic villi), which has a genetic makeup identical to the fetus's. A pre-CVS ultrasound is performed. Then, in the standard vaginal CVS, you lie on an exam table as you would for a pelvic exam. Your cervix and vagina are cleansed, then the cervix is grasped with a tonglike instrument that holds it steady during the procedure. A catheter (thin plastic tube) is then threaded through the vagina and cervix into the chorionic villi. A small amount of villi is suctioned into a syringe. The entire procedure may only take a few minutes, but in some cases more than one attempt at catheter insertion is necessary, or, if your uterus begins to spasm (which is common and normal), the procedure may have to be postponed until another time. Some women find CVS extremely painful (since the clamp on the cervix can cause cramping sensations), while others only find it moderately uncomfortable. The procedure for a transabdominal CVS is almost identical to amniocentesis, except that villi are extracted, not amniotic fluid.

Results: Usually available within one week as compared to an average of three weeks with amniocentesis

Accuracy: Definitive study results on CVS's accuracy are not yet in. So far, however, CVS seems to be nearly as accurate as amniocentesis.

Risks: Miscarriages occur in about 2 percent of CVS patients as compared to about 1 percent of those who have had amniocentesis. This difference is considered statistically insignificant, however. And since the majority of losses do not occur in the first few days following CVS, many experts conjecture that many of the miscarriages are due to natural causes and not to the procedure. Still, CVS has only been in use for about five years (as compared to twenty for amnio) and the final answers on potential risks/complications are not in yet.

Alpha-Fetoprotein Testing (AFT)

Timing: Fifteen to eighteen weeks

Purpose: Screens for neural-tube defects (NTD). One to two babies in every thousand are born in this country with an NTD in which the tissues that form the brain and spine do not close properly. Ninety-five percent of NTDs occur in families with *no* prior history of the defect.

Procedure: It's a simple blood test. If you are planning on having CVS or amniocentesis, NTD testing will be done on the villi or amniotic fluid, making the AFT blood test unnecessary.

Results: Available within one week

Accuracy: The test is oversensitive: fifty out of each one thousand women will have an abnormal result, yet only one or two of these women will actually have an affected fetus. The test can also miss defects, up to 10 to 20 percent according to some estimates. What's important to remember: the blood test does not definitively *diagnose* NTDs—it's only a screening procedure that aims to identify those who *might* be at risk.

Risks: Since the test frequently indicates that there is a problem when there is none, a positive reading can cause weeks of unnecessary agony and uncertainty. To rule out a false positive reading, a second AFT blood test is done; if the second blood test isn't normal, an ultrasound examination is done to see if there are two or more fetuses or if the pregnancy is more advanced than was previously thought—the two most common reasons that account for a false positive result. If ultrasound doesn't yield definitive information, the next step is amniocentesis.

Percutaneous Umbilical Blood Sampling (PUBS)

Timing: Eighteen to thirty-six weeks

Purpose: To confirm amniocentesis results; to test for fetal exposure to an infectious disease (such as German measles); to pinpoint causes of slow fetal growth late in a pregnancy.

Procedure: Almost identical to amnio, except a fine needle is guided into a blood vessel of the umbilical cord, from which fetal blood is then obtained.

Results: Usually available in three days

Accuracy: Although there is no definitive research on the accuracy of PUBS, since the procedure is still quite new and experimental, it is believed to be highly accurate.

Risks: Carries the same risks as amnio, plus a slight additional risk of premature labor, premature rupture of membranes, and clotting in the umbilical cord

---

ৰ KEEPING CLEAR ON THE SUBJECT OF BIRTH DEFECTS ৰ

It's always important to keep your eyes on the flip side of a statistic. For instance, the statistic that 2 to 3 percent of all babies are born with some type of major birth defect means that at least 97 percent of all babies *aren't* born with one. It's important to remind yourself that serious disabilities are relatively rare and to keep in mind that the chances of your baby experiencing a problem are, in all likelihood, relatively low.

Even couples labeled "high risk" for having a child with a birth defect need to remember that the label doesn't necessarily mean that their child will be born with one. Many couples in the "high-risk" category can and do have normal, healthy children. Of course, it's essential to be well informed about the subject of birth defects, but it's essential, too, to keep the right perspective and to remember how much room for optimism there really is.

ৰ *Your Diet*

FOOD AVERSIONS AND FOOD CRAVINGS

There are countless theories about why pregnant women suddenly crave particular foods and why they suddenly are repelled by ones they previously loved. These theories, however, have yet to hold up under scientific scrutiny. The most popular hypothesis, that cravings signal a nutritional need and aversions a warning, is almost unanimously rejected by experts. It's not thought, in other words, that a craving for pickles and ice cream signals a need for salt and calcium. Nor is it believed that an aversion to red meat, for example, means red meat is somehow dangerous or potentially harmful.

Whatever their purpose, dietary cravings and aversions are quite common during pregnancy, especially in the first six months.

Some women also experience strange tastes in their mouths and find they are unusually sensitive to the smells of certain foods.

As a general rule, there's no danger in following your yen as long as you're not one of the rare women who crave nonfood substances, such as clay, dirt, detergent, or chalk, and as long as your cravings don't lead you to eat a diet that is overly extreme. A diet exclusively based on cookies and cake, for instance, wouldn't supply your baby with the proper nutrients and would cause you to gain an unhealthy amount of weight. But a fast-food burger or candy bar—two foods many women seem to crave— now and then won't compromise your health or your baby's.

In the same way, following your aversions is fine, if doing so doesn't compromise the overall healthfulness of your diet. But many women find they have a hard time stomaching milk and/or meat, the two best sources of calcium and protein. Although it's harder to get enough of these nutrients from other foods, it's not impossible. For alternatives to milk, see pp. 103–04, and to meat, see pp. 90–93.

﹩ *Your Workout*

EXERCISES TO RELIEVE HEAD AND SHOULDER STRAIN

The two exercises described here are designed to sooth stressed shoulder and neck muscles, muscles some women find get strained as their breasts get heavier. Learning how to ease upper body soreness can also be valuable during labor, when shoulder and neck muscles frequently become tense and achy from anticipation of contraction pain; it can be useful postpartum, too, when shoulder and neck muscles can easily get taxed from carrying a baby in a front body carrier (like a Snugli).

Shoulder De-Tenser

Stand with your feet slightly apart, arms hanging loosely at your sides. Slowly rotate your right shoulder backward in a circle three times, then forward three times. Repeat with the left shoulder. Then lift both shoulders, rotate backward, then forward, three times in each direction. This exercise feels particularly relaxing after you've been hunched over a desk, computer, or typewriter for a long stretch.

Neck Relaxer

Sit up straight in a comfortable chair. Let your chin drop toward your chest. As you gently and slowly rotate your head to the right, hold the following three positions to the count of five: your right ear parallel to your right shoulder; your left ear parallel to your left shoulder; your chin dropped toward your chest again. Repeat, rotating in the opposite direction and making sure to keep your shoulders loose, not hunched up. This exercise is the most soothing if you do it with your eyes shut, in a quiet room.

❧ *Your Feelings*

THE PSYCHOLOGICAL SIDE OF PRENATAL TESTING

Choosing or refusing to test is an intensely personal decision—so much so that no two couples are likely to view the pros and cons in exactly the same way. For example, some couples know they would never consider an abortion even if the baby had a disability and so decide not to test. Other couples, equally as sure they would never opt for terminating the pregnancy, choose to test because they feel knowing about problems in advance would help prepare them for the delivery and the baby's needs after birth.

When you decide not to test, your feelings as you go through pregnancy are likely to be similar to the emotions pregnant women have experienced for millennia: on some days, you will be convinced that your baby is normal and you'll find joy and reassurance in the fact that the majority of babies are in fact born normal. On yet other days—the dark days—you may worry and conjure up fears about health problems or handicaps. Especially when you're in the grip of these worries about the baby's state of being, you may find yourself feeling ambivalent, even guilty, about your decision not to test. In addition, you may at times be made to feel defensive about the choice you've made, as many people feel you "owe it" to yourself to take advantage of available technology.

The choice to test can also put you on an emotional roller coaster, even when you don't expect it to.

I opted for amniocentesis without much protracted delibera-tion; it was something my husband felt strongly about me having, and I had a "why not" attitude toward it. Yet what seemed like a simple medical choice turned out to have deep emotional con-sequences. I found I became quite reluctant to personalize or visualize my baby before the procedure: I was hesitant to become too "attached." Announcing and talking about the pregnancy also made me extremely nervous: I was afraid, even a little superstitious, to think of the pregnancy as "real" until I knew the amnio results.

As the day of the procedure approached, my fears grew. I knew that in a small percentage of women ultrasound prior to the amnio reveals either a gross defect or a miscarriage in progress, so for days in advance I braced myself for discovering the worst. (I was so relieved and thrilled to see a whole, lively baby on the ultrasound screen that my fears about a needle entering my stomach almost completely diminished—I found the physical aspects of the procedure quite easy to get through.)

But the worst part of the amnio process turned out to be the three weeks' wait for the results. I couldn't stop myself from contemplating problems. More than once I wished I hadn't had the test. I felt incapable of terminating the pregnancy (the action my husband and I had agreed upon) if the news was bad. Other times I felt coolly "rational," reasoning that even though termi-nating the pregnancy at this point would be horrific, a lifetime coping with a child with severe birth defects would be more difficult—medically, financially, and emotionally. All in all, the weeks of waiting for the results were emotionally draining. So much so, that when the geneticist finally called with the results, I simply burst into tears over the phone when I received the news that the baby was fine. I was completely overcome with relief and joy.

Would I opt for amniocentesis again, in a next pregnancy? On the one hand, despite the anxiety it provoked during the first half of my pregnancy, it had a tremendously positive impact on the second half, liberating me from my deepest fears. Still, I'm not 100 percent certain I would choose it again. I am sure, however, that I would give the decision to test or not to test a lot more consideration than I did the first time around.

WHEN THE NEWS IS BAD

Support from friends and family is an invaluable comfort when you are confronted with an abnormal prenatal diagnosis. But you should also expect to get strong, solid counseling from your doctor and genetic counselor.

If a test result leads you to end the pregnancy, you may want to write for the booklet "Difficult Decisions for Families Whose Unborn Baby Has a Serious Problem" (The Centering Corporation, Dr. S. M. Johnson, Box 3367, Omaha, NE 68103; 402-553-1200).

If you and your partner decide to continue the pregnancy in spite of genetic problems, you'll want to contact an organization familiar with the specific defect diagnosed (such as the National Down Syndrome Society or the Spina Bifida Association of America). Voluntary organizations not only provide you with educational material and medical information about a defect, but they can often put you in contact with parents who are raising children with similar disabilities. You can locate the organization that may be most helpful to you by referring to *Reaching Out: A Directory of Voluntary Organizations in Maternal and Child Health* (published by the National Center for Education in Maternal and Child Health, 8201 Greensborough Drive, Suite 600, McLean, VA 22102). Your doctor or genetic counselor is likely to have a copy.

ᦉ *Your Life-Style*

AVOIDING LYME DISEASE

If you'll be pregnant during the summer months (June through August), you'll want to take special precautions to avoid contracting lyme disease, a bacterial infection spread by ticks that preliminary research suggests could raise the risk of miscarriage and birth defects if left untreated.

Lyme disease is largely a threat in Northeastern states (Massachusetts, Rhode Island, Connecticut, New York, New Jersey), parts of the upper Midwest (especially Wisconsin and Minnesota), and the northern Pacific Coast (particularly California and Oregon), areas where the Ixodes dammini tick (often called the deer tick) is prevalent. The Ixodes dammini tick is about the size of a pin head, much, much smaller than the more common wood or dog tick, which does *not* transmit the infection.

Spotting symptoms. Because the Ixodes dammini tick is so tiny, you may not even realize you've been bitten, so you need to be on the alert for early symptoms which may occur anywhere from a week to a month after a bite. In at least 50 percent of all cases, the first sign of the disease is a bull's-eye rash, which is generally neither painful nor itchy and lasts about three to four weeks. Flulike reactions—chills, headache, slight fever, swollen lymph glands, reddened eyes, fatigue—can also be early signs of the infection and may occur even if you don't get the telltale rash.

What to do. If you are worried that you may have contracted lyme disease, you should see a doctor immediately, preferably one skilled at detecting the disease (your state health department can help you locate a physician with experience in treating lyme disease, or you can contact the International Lyme Borreliosis Foundation Inc., P.O. Box 462, Tolland, CT 06804, 203-871-2900, for help).

You should also get a blood test, although this frequently yields a false negative result. Because both the test and many labs can be unreliable, experts recommend you have several blood tests, analyzed by several different laboratories. If any of the results are positive, it is likely you've been infected.

Treating lyme disease in a pregnant woman demands prompt, aggressive action. Medication must be strong enough to cross the placenta and kill the infection before it has a chance to do any damage to the fetus. That's why most experts recommend you undergo two weeks of intravenous therapy with antibiotics (if you weren't pregnant, most doctors would prescribe a two-week course of orally administered penicillin or tetracycline). When treated intravenously, mothers exposed to lyme disease deliver babies who appear to be perfectly normal and unharmed by the infection. Although the data is still scarce and sketchy, it appears that serious complications are only likely to occur when the disease goes untreated.

Prevention. Obviously, avoiding tick bites is the best way to ensure that you and your unborn baby are not at risk for lyme disease. And you can reduce your chances of being bitten with these tactics:

• Avoid trailblazing through tall grassy or wooded areas where deer (which carry and spread the ticks) also roam.
• When in a tick-infested area, wear light-colored clothing (so ticks are easy to spot), long-sleeved shirts, long pants, and shoes and socks (not sandals). Tuck your shirt into your pants, and your pants legs into your socks, so ticks can't get under clothing to skin.
• After being outdoors, check your clothes carefully for ticks; shower and check your hair and body well, too.
• Inspect your dog or cat for ticks every night—don't count on tick collars being effective. Also, keep pets off furniture, especially beds.
• Although they can be effective at keeping ticks at bay, avoid heavy use of insect repellents, since their poisons can be absorbed by your skin. Apply repellents only on clothes, not directly on skin.
• If you find a tick on you, remove it gently with tweezers, then save it for inspection (by a doctor) by putting it in a jar of alcohol, labeled with the date and site of the bite. Clean the bite areas with a liberal amount of rubbing alcohol. Remember, not all ticks carry the disease, so there's no need to panic. But it does make sense to contact a physician with special knowledge of lyme disease to discuss possible courses of action.

Everyone has about a 1 in 250 chance of bearing identical twins—twins that are formed when a single fertilized egg divides into two embryos. Identical twins, which mirror each other genetically and so are always the same sex and always look alike, seem to occur randomly; no woman is more likely to bear identical twins than another.

The chances of bearing fraternal twins—those formed when two separate eggs are fertilized by two separate sperm—are estimated to be between one in eighty to one in one hundred for the majority of women. But your chances may be greater if:

• You are black. It's estimated that roughly one out of every seventy black women have twins in the U.S.

• Your mother was a fraternal twin. Twins run in families, with the trait passed on in maternal genes.

• You are between thirty-five and thirty-nine years old. It's speculated that as a woman ages she releases more than one egg during ovulation; once past forty though, most women begin to release fewer eggs.

• You have already borne several children.

• You conceived after recently going off the Pill. It seems that after some women stop taking the Pill, they experience a surge of hormones that stimulate more than one egg to be released.

• You conceived with the help of a fertility drug. Seven to nine percent of women who take Clomid conceive twins; the multiple birth rate may be as high as 20 percent with Pergonal.

• You conceived via in-vitro fertilization (IVF) or gamete intrafallopian transfer (GIFT). With both these techniques the odds are high that several eggs will get fertilized and implant.

These days, most multiple births are diagnosed well before delivery. As early as eight weeks into a pregnancy, an obstetrician/gynecologist may begin to be suspicious if you are gaining weight at an unusually high rate and/or the height of your uterus is expanding at a faster than usual pace. An ultrasound examination can definitively confirm whether you are carrying twins; ultrasound is also quite accurate in determining triplets, quadruplets, etc., although in rare cases it fails to detect a fetus.

Problems in Plural Pregnancies

Women carrying multiple fetuses tend to experience the common discomforts of pregnancy, such as nausea, fatigue, heartburn, indigestion, swelling, and breathlessness, far more intensely than women carrying singletons. They also have a higher risk of suffering from anemia, preeclampsia, and gestational diabetes. Because as many as 50 percent of all twin pregnancies result in delivery four weeks early (with triplets born, on average, eight weeks early, and quadruplets even earlier, at minus twelve weeks), most doctors try to delay the onset of labor by advising women with multiple fetuses to restrict their activities and increase their bed rest in the last trimester. Giving birth to multiple fetuses is also more complicated; almost 50 percent are delivered by cesarean section.

There's a wealth of resources a woman carrying more than one fetus can tap for information on multiple pregnancy, birth, breast-feeding, and baby development. The two following support organizations will provide you with information about twin-care books and research centers; they also produce newsletters and other written material on all aspects of multiple-baby care and development.

Twin Services
P.O. Box 10066
Berkeley, CA 94709
415-524-0863

National Organization of Mothers of Twin Clubs, Inc.
P.O. Box 23188
Albuquerque, NM 87921-1188
505-275-0955

5

MONTH FOUR
(13½ TO 18 WEEKS)

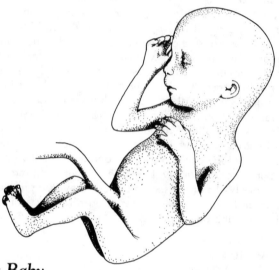

✌ *Your Baby*

WEIGHT: 8 ounces
LENGTH: 6 to 7 inches

From this month on, development is mostly a matter of matura-
tion and refinement, since all the fetus's major organs are already
formed. If the fetus is a girl, for instance, she already has a completed formed uterus, two differentiated ovaries, even rudimentary follicles containing ovum. A boy fetus already has ducts that
will someday convey sperm, although the testes don't begin to
descend into the scrotum until after twenty-eight weeks.

The following "finishing touches" are applied in the fourth
month: To the fetus's fingertips are added nails as well as the

whorls and grooves that make up an individual's unique fingerprints. Its hairline or pattern of scalp hair is established. Lower limbs reach their final relative proportions, and the fetus's hands gain the ability to grasp. Finally, the fetus's bones calcify or harden to such a degree that they would be detectable if X-rayed at this point.

❧ Your Body

COMMON MINOR DISCOMFORTS

The pregnancy side effects described ahead often crop up in the second trimester or later.

Urinary Tract Infections (UTI). Urinary tract infections are one of the most common discomforts of pregnancy; it is estimated that one out of every ten expectant women is plagued with one sometime during her nine months.

There appear to be two reasons why pregnancy makes you more prone to UTIs. Since the bladder lies directly in front of the uterus, it is increasingly compressed as the uterus enlarges. This compression keeps the bladder from emptying completely. Thus, urine is left sitting in the urinary tract to "stagnate," a situation that encourages bacteria to thrive and multiply.

Change in the actual chemical composition of your urine is a factor, too. During pregnancy, urine contains higher levels of estrogen and glucose. This makes urine less acidic and consequently an even better medium for bacteria.

There are basically two types of UTIs. Cystitis, an infection that is confined to the lower urinary tract (the bladder and urethra), sparks these symptoms: a frequent urge to urinate, although you may only be able to pass a few drops of urine at a time; a sharp pain or burning sensation when you urinate; and/or an achy feeling just above your pubic bone, in your back or sides.

The more severe UTI, pyelonephritis, is an infection that has traveled to your kidneys and is characterized by high fever, chills, nausea, and vomiting, and may also include the symptoms of cystitis. Pyelonephritis is particularly dangerous during pregnancy since it may trigger premature labor. That is why most obstetrician/gynecologists perform urinalysis on your first visit; if you have a high bacteria count—which could put you at risk for developing a kidney infection later—UTI treatment is begun before a problem can set in.

Treating both cystitis and pyelonephritis involves taking a course of antibiotics. Ideally, you want to avoid taking medications during pregnancy, but in this case the remedy is less of a hazard than allowing the condition to go unchecked. You should always contact your doctor when you feel the first signs of a UTI. Unfortunately, women who have had a round with a UTI tend to be prone to recurrent bouts. But you may be able to avoid repeated infections (and having to repeatedly take courses of antibiotics) by following these simple preventive steps:

• Drink plenty of liquids (a total of six to eight glasses of water and vitamin C–rich juice a day) to flush bacteria out of your urinary tract. Vitamin C may help keep your urine more acidic, thus less welcoming to bacteria.

• Wear cotton underwear. Synthetics don't "breathe" and so can make it easier for bacteria to thrive.

• Wipe front to back after a bowel movement to prevent bacteria from the intestinal tract from entering and infecting the urinary one.

• Void frequently to prevent urine from stagnating.

• Wash your genital area and empty your bladder both before and after intercourse to prevent bacteria from traveling up into the urethra.

Increased vaginal discharge. Due to the amount of increased blood supply to your vagina and cervix, the amount of vaginal discharge you have will tend to increase as your pregnancy progresses. In fact, you may find your discharge becomes so profuse that you'll want to wear panty liners or change your underwear more than once a day (never douche during pregnancy, though, unless you have your doctor's okay).

You'll know your discharge, although abundant, is healthy and normal if it's whitish clear, mild in odor, and otherwise produces no symptoms. In contrast, unhealthy discharges—ones that signal the presence of an infection—are distinguished by these features: 1. A thick, white, curdy discharge that's itchy and odorless. Caused by *Candida albicans*, this yeast infection can be transferred to the baby's mouth as he or she passes through the birth canal. 2. A profuse, greenish discharge usually accompanied by burning and a need to urinate frequently. Caused by the gonococcus organism, gonorrhea can also be passed to the baby at birth, causing permanent blindness if not treated promptly. 3. A yellowish, foamy, itchy discharge with an unpleasant odor. Caused by *Trichomonas vaginalis*, this infection is primarily a nuisance to you, not a threat to your baby. 4. A heavy discharge accompanied by burning during urination and a tender sensation in the lower pelvic region. This could be a chlamydia infection, which can increase the risk of premature labor and amniotic-fluid infection. Call your doctor promptly if your discharge has any of the features characteristic of an infection. Even if you *think* your discharge is normal but aren't completely sure, it's best to play it safe and see your doctor.

Bleeding gums. During pregnancy, estrogen softens your gums, while the increase in blood volume may make them swell a bit. The result can be gums that easily bleed when you brush your teeth or bite into firm foods.

You can't reverse this problem totally, but you can prevent it from worsening by cleaning and flossing teeth carefully and regularly. Proper dental hygiene keeps plaque from accumulating, which can further irritate your gums, and helps reduce the risk of your contracting gum (periodontal) disease.

In addition to good daily care of teeth, it helps to steer clear of sugary, sticky foods that encourage plaque buildup. You should also see your dentist at least once during your pregnancy for a thorough cleaning and checkup (but postpone any restorative work that requires you to have X rays or anesthesia other than novocaine).

Nasal Congestion. A stuffy nose and frequent nosebleeds are pregnancy side effects caused by the increase in blood volume and hormonal activity.

To treat a stuffy nose, try a natural or saline nasal spray (available in health-food stores) or invest in a humidifier. Although some drugstore nasal sprays, antihistamines, and decongestants appear to be safe to use during pregnancy, it's best to consult with your doctor before self-medicating.

To stop a nosebleed, simply grasp the soft, outer part of your nose firmly between your thumb and index finger and hold it for several minutes. Don't lie down, since that could cause blood to trickle down your throat, possibly making you vomit. You can also dab some witch hazel (which is in effective astringent) on the bleeding area or insert a cotton ball soaked with fresh lemon juice (also an astringent) into the nostril for several minutes.

≈ Your Doctor Appointment

ROUTINE CHECKS

From now on, every visit to your doctor will include these two tests:

- Fetal heartbeat. A few practitioners still rely on the stethoscope to detect the fetus's heartbeat and to confirm that the heart rate is normal, but most now use the Doppler probe, a small hand-held device that works via ultrasound vibrations. With the Doppler probe you can hear the sound of your baby's heart beating, too.
- Uterus size. Most doctors keep track of the growth of your uterus by measuring the distance from your pubic bone to the top of your uterus, using a measuring tape with centimeter markers. If the uterus appears to be growing faster than usual (which might mean you are carrying twins) or slower than normal (which may only mean your baby is healthy, but on the small side) your doctor will probably want you to have an ultrasound examination to check your baby's progress. In the last month of pregnancy, however, it's quite normal for the height of your uterus to stop increasing or even decrease as your baby's head drops down and engages in your pelvis.

≈ Your Diet

MEETING PROTEIN NEEDS WITHOUT MEAT

You need to get at least seventy-five grams of protein daily during pregnancy. If you regularly include meat, poultry, fish, eggs, and dairy products in your diet, it's easy to get this amount of protein without much thought. But if you are a vegetarian or you have an aversion to meat, poultry, and fish for a prolonged period of time, you'll need to pay attention to getting adequate protein.

Unlike the protein you get from animal foods, plant protein is incomplete; it lacks the full array of essential amino acids that your body needs in order to be able to utilize it fully. But plant foods can be combined to create properly balanced, complete proteins: legumes with grains, legumes with nuts and seeds, as well as dairy products or eggs with any vegetable protein can be combined to form complete proteins.

It's possible to safely meet your pregnancy protein needs as well as get an adequate supply of vitamins and minerals when you include eggs and dairy products in your vegetarian diet. It's not advisable to exclude dairy products and eggs during pregnancy, since it's extremely hard to obtain enough vitamins and minerals, protein and calories to properly fuel fetal growth without them.

The following three charts are adapted from *Jane Brody's Nutrition Book* (W. W. Norton & Co., 1981, New York); they illustrate the principles involved in getting enough balanced protein in meatless meals.

VEGETARIAN DISHES WITH COMPLETE PROTEIN

Grains with Legumes

Rice with lentils
Rice with black-eyed peas
Peanut-butter sandwich

Macaroni enriched with soy
   flour
Bean soup with toast
Falafel (chick-pea pancake)
   with pita bread

Grains with Milk

Oatmeal with milk
Wheat flakes with milk
Rice pudding
Pancakes and waffles
Breads and muffins made
   with milk
Pizza

Macaroni and cheese
Cheese sandwich
Creamed soup with noodles or
   rice
Quiche
Meatless lasagna
Granola with milk

Legumes with Seeds

Bean curd with sesame seeds
Hummus (chick-pea and
   sesame paste)

Bean soup with sesame meal

Grains with Eggs

Rice pudding
Kasha (buckwheat groats)
Fried rice
Oatmeal cookies
Quiche

Egg-salad sandwich
Spaghetti pancake
Noodle pudding

Other Vegetables with Milk or Eggs

Potato salad
Mashed potatoes with milk
Eggplant Parmesan
Broccoli with cheese sauce
Cream of pumpkin soup

Cheese and potato soup
Vegetable omelet
Scalloped potatoes
Spinach salad with sliced egg

VEGETABLE PROTEIN FOODS

When you combine any of the legumes in the center column with any of the foods in the right or left columns, you create a complete protein.

Grains	Legumes	Seeds and Nuts
Barley	Beans (black,	Pumpkin
Buckwheat	broad, kidney,	Sesame
Bulgur	lima, mung,	Squash
Corn	navy, pea, soy)	Sunflower
Millet	Black-eyed peas	Almonds
Oats	(cowpeas)	Brazil Nuts
Rice	Chick-peas	Cashews
Triticale	(garbanzos)	Coconuts
Wheat	Peanuts	Filberts
	Peas	Macadamia Nuts
		Pecans
		Pine Nuts
		Pistachio Nuts
		Walnuts

How to Get Enough Balanced Protein During Pregnancy

Each of the meals listed below supplies about eighteen grams of protein. So if you ate three of these meals, and drank your quart of milk, you would easily meet the pregnancy protein requirement of seventy-five grams of protein daily. (Three of the meals below provide a total of fifty-four grams of protein, and a quart of milk provides another thirty-two grams, making for a total of eighty-six grams).

Food Combination	Amount	Protein (g)
Peanut butter	3 tablespoons	12.0
Whole-wheat bread	2 slices	5.2
Soybean curd (tofu)	1 piece (4.2 ounces)	9.4
Soybean sprouts	1 cup	6.5
Sesame seeds	2 tablespoons	3.0
Lentils	1 cup	15.6
Brown rice	½ cup	2.6
Split-pea soup	¾ cup cooked peas	12.0
Brown rice	½ cup	2.5
Whole-wheat bread	1 slice	2.6
Macaroni	1 cup	6.5
Cheddar cheese	1½ ounces	10.6
Roll (brown-and-serve)	1 roll	2.2
Kasha (buckwheat groats)	1 cup	8.0
Egg	1 large	6.5
Potato (baked)	7 ounces	4.0
Egg noodles	½ cup	3.3
Cottage cheese (creamed)	½ cup	14.3
Oatmeal made with milk	1 cup cooked	4.8
Whole-wheat toast	2 slices	5.2

❧ *Your Workout*

AN EXERCISE TO CUT DOWN ON CALF CRAMPS

During the second half of pregnancy, it's not uncommon to wake up in the middle of the night with your calf muscle seized up in a painful knot. The precise cause of these leg cramps isn't known, although it seems likely that they are due to a pinched nerve (what triggers the nerve to become pinched in the first place is likely to be a combination of your expanding uterus pressing on nerves and the tossing and turning during sleep).

When you are actually experiencing a calf cramp, the best thing to do is bend your toes toward your head in a gentle stretch; don't point your toes since that can make the spasm worse. Most

Cramp cutter: 1. Stand facing a wall, feet about one foot apart, arms straight out, palms against the wall. 2. Keeping your feet flat on the floor and your body straight, bend your elbows and touch your nose to the wall. Push back to the starting position. Repeat at least ten times. (If you don't feel the stretch in your calves, move your legs farther away from the wall. Whenever you want to increase the stretch, just move farther from the wall.)

cramps will pass as you stretch. If a cramp does not ease up, bend your knee, directing your toes toward your body, then knead the knotted muscle (by squeezing and releasing it every few seconds) to help it relax.

The exercise illustrated at left serves to stretch calf muscles and, in doing so, helps prevent cramps (since relaxed, loose muscles are less likely to contract and go into spasm). Try to do the exercise before going to bed every night.

≥● *Your Feelings*

QUICKENING: TO REACH THE STAGE OF GESTATION AT WHICH FETAL MOTION IS FELT

As you wait for the time when you'll start to feel your baby move, it's not uncommon to become a little anxious, to worry, "Why haven't I felt anything yet?" It helps to keep the following two things in mind. First, while some women feel fetal movements as early as fourteen weeks, most mothers-to-be (especially first-time mothers) only discern movements after eighteen or twenty-one weeks (or even as late as twenty-six weeks). Second, it's not always easy to recognize first fetal movements, since early movements are not usually experienced as distinct jabs or kicks but indistinct, vague "flutterings" or sinking sensations that are easy to mistake for digestive rumblings. In other words, feeling your baby's first movements may not be a clearly demarcated "event" for you but a series of suspicions ("I think that was the baby moving") that finally add up to certainty.

Once you're sure you're feeling the baby (and that may take weeks after the first suspicion), chances are you'll be excited and reassured. The baby is likely to somehow seem more "real" to you from then on. Most women also find that their feelings toward their unborn baby greatly intensify once movements are felt, and that the movements are, overall, a source of joy and comfort during the latter part of the pregnancy. There may still be times, however, when the subject of the baby's movements cause you concern. These facts should provide perspective:

• Every baby has his or her own unique pattern of movement: some kick like clockwork the same time everyday, others jab you irregularly; some pack powerful punches, others just nudge you gently. That means if a friend describes fetal kicks so strong that they wake her up in the middle of the night, you shouldn't be worried if you only feel gentle pushes. You simply can't compare your baby's style of "getting around" with any other baby's. The range of what's normal, usual, and healthy is tremendously wide.

• When you are active, you'll tend to notice your baby's movements less and your baby will tend to move less (as he or she is lulled by the rhythm of your movements). Also, there will be days when your baby is more wakeful and active than others.

• In a normal, low-risk pregnancy there's generally no need to count fetal movements every day (in some high-risk pregnancies, doctors will instruct a woman to count fetal movements three times a day in thirty-minute sessions). After the thirtieth week, though, you should contact your doctor if you feel no fetal activity or feel markedly diminished activity in any twenty-four–hour period. Even if you feel no movement or a slowing, it doesn't necessarily mean something is wrong; if you're near term, for instance, a lessening in activity is often a signal that labor is about to begin.

ᨒ Your Life-Style

PLANNING YOUR MATERNITY LEAVE

Before making any decisions, first find out what your company's maternity-leave policy is. You'll want to know the answers to the following questions:

• What is the maximum time I can take off with pay?
• Can I use vacation and/or personal time to extend paid leave?
• What is the maximum time I can take off without pay?
• Can I return to the same job? Can I return to a different job?
• Can I return part-time?
• Is flexible scheduling a possibility?
• Is job-sharing possible?
• Can I work at home, either full- or part-time?
• Can I bring my baby to work?

Obviously, the more valuable you are as an employee, the more motivation your boss will have to respond with flexibility to your requests. Also, the type of organization you work for will play a big part in determining what kind of options you might have open to you; some businesses have quite liberal, creative leave policies, while others have quite "uncooperative," rigid ones.

The law does not require an employer to offer a specific number of weeks for maternity leave. But the Pregnancy Discrimination Act (PDA) does require employers who maintain disability policies or who offer medical leaves-of-absence to include pregnancy among the covered disabilities. The PDA also states that an employer can't penalize you because of pregnancy, which means your accumulated seniority, accrued retirement benefits, and salary level must be reinstated when you return to work. In addition, a number of states have laws and regulations governing parental leave; you should check with your state's department of labor or human and civil rights agencies for information about them. Also, if you have questions about your work situation and legal rights, a good resource to tap is the 9 to 5 Office Survival Hotline set up by the National Association of Working Women (800-245-9865, 10 A.M.–4 P.M. EST; in Cleveland, 216-566-5420).

Once you have a sense of what your options might be, you need to consider what you want and need. You'll want to ask yourself:

- For how long can I afford not to work?
- What will childcare cost me if I return to work?
- Can I live on a smaller amount of money if I work less or part-time?
- Would taking off a big block of time now adversely affect my career? Would I resent that?
- How satisfied am I with my present job? Would quitting and reentering the workplace in a new job be a viable alternative?
- Is freelancing a possibility—could I make money doing it and would I like it?
- Am I likely to be happier not returning to work or returning

to work (keeping in mind that most women feel some conflict about the two choices).

If this is your first child, you may not really know the answers to many of these questions, since it can be hard to predict how you'll feel after your baby is born. Many women, for example, are surprised to discover that they have no desire whatsoever to leave their babies to return to work, while others find they miss their work connections and discover staying at home isn't what they thought it would be. That's why it makes the most sense to avoid taking any "radical" course, such as quitting or insisting you'll be back to work after a minimum of time off, until after your baby is born, when you know how you feel.

6

MONTH FIVE

(18 to 22½ WEEKS)

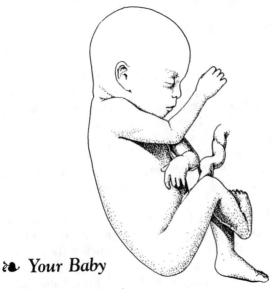

🐚 *Your Baby*

WEIGHT: 1 pound
LENGTH: 9 inches

At this, the halfway point in your pregnancy, the fetus takes a "rest." Growth is slow and undramatic, especially when compared to the phenomenal transformations that occurred in the first trimester.

During this "rest" period, the most notable development is in the skin. Oil glands appear and begin producing a fatty material called vernix caseosa, which coats the fetus's skin and serves to protect it from getting waterlogged, scratched, or chapped. The skin also acquires functional hair follicles: eyebrows, head hair,

and a fine downy body hair called lanugo begin to grow. But in
appearance, the fetus's skin is still quite wrinkled and translucent. That's because there is, as yet, little underlying fat to
plump it up and smooth it out.

➣ *Your Body*

CHANGES IN YOUR SKIN

Hormones, particularly estrogen, affect your skin. So it's no
wonder that pregnancy can stimulate a wide range of changes in
body and facial skin. You'll probably notice at least some of these
conditions:

- *New mole growth.* It's normal to develop new moles (nevi)
or freckles and for existing moles to enlarge and darken. These
moles can be smooth and flat, raised and bumpy, red, tan, brown,
or almost black in color. They sometimes disappear by six
months postpartum; if they don't they can easily be removed by a
dermatologist. (If a mole is itchy, painful, inflamed, oozy, bloody,
or includes a variety of shades, there's a chance it could be
precancerous and should be evaluated immediately by a dermatologist).
- *Skin tags.* These are tiny little flaps of loose skin that often
appear on your neck or underarms. They sometimes fall off by
themselves a few months after you've given birth; if they don't,
they can be removed by a dermatologist.
- *Pigmentation.* The darker complexioned you are, the more
you'll notice a darkening of your skin on the inside of your upper
thighs, the area surrounding your nipples (areola), and in your
navel. You'll also find that your linea alba—the vertical line that
extends from your belly button to your pubic hair—darkens (and
thus becomes the linea negra); it may even extend past your
navel, up toward your breasts. In fair-complexioned women,
these pigment changes will disappear almost completely postpartum, but if you're dark-skinned they may be permanent, although
they will fade a little with time.
- *Facial flush.* Your face may be infused with a glow or
rosiness due to the increase in blood volume. The flush, one of
pregnancy's best side effects, generally begins to be apparent by

month five (but often surfaces even earlier, in month three or four).

- **Mask of Pregnancy** (melasma). This is a splotchy and irregular darkening that usually develops on the forehead, cheeks, temples, and upper lip. It usually disappears or considerably lightens a few months after delivery. Using sunscreen or avoiding the sun during pregnancy may prevent it from occurring.

- **Stretch marks** (striae gravidarum). These characteristically appear on your lower abdomen and breasts. Unfortunately, they don't disappear after birth, but they will become less obvious, fading from a pinkish or purplish hue to a faint, white sheen.

- **Spider veins** (angiomas). New, little capillaries, which look like red or purple squiggles right below the skin's surface, often pop up on your breasts, stomach, and thighs. They typically vanish a few weeks after childbirth.

- **Inflamed palms.** Sometimes because of changes in your circulation, the skin on your palms and the ball of your thumb gets red and inflamed. Postpartum, it goes back to normal.

- **Breakouts.** Even if you've always had clear skin, you may experience breakouts at some point in pregnancy. If you're acne-prone, pregnancy can affect it positively or negatively—it's unpredictable. One common pattern is that the acne will first get worse, then start to improve around the fourth or fifth month. Be sure to avoid antibiotic treatments and Accutane, which can cause birth defects. Check with your doctor before using any topical treatments, including over-the-counter ones.

- **Itching.** Dry, itchy skin is a common pregnancy complaint. In particular, many women find that their stomach skin itches (probably because this skin gets so stretched and taut). Using a moisturizer may give you some relief; avoiding harsh soaps and hot water, which strip skin of its natural oils, should also help.

❧ Your Doctor Appointment

WHY YOUR BLOOD PRESSURE
IS CHECKED AT EVERY VISIT

Pregnancy-induced high blood pressure (preeclampsia) is one of the most common complications of pregnancy, affecting an estimated seven out of every one hundred pregnant women. What causes the condition or why some women get it and others don't is still largely a mystery. It is known, however, that several classes of women are most at risk: those experiencing their first pregnancy, women who are under eighteen or over thirty-five, overweight women, diabetics, women who have had kidney disease, or women who are carrying more than one fetus.

Preeclampsia can develop anytime after the twentieth week of pregnancy, although it most commonly occurs later, after twenty-eight weeks. Its hallmark is a notable increase in blood pressure. To detect this rise as early as possible is the reason why your doctor checks and tracks your blood pressure at each visit. If the increase is mild, you may have no symptoms whatsoever; you probably won't even suspect you have high blood pressure until your doctor discovers it. In more severe cases, the warning signs are swelling (edema), particularly of the face and fingers, a sudden weight gain (anything more than two pounds in one week), headaches, and/or eyesight problems.

If untreated, preeclampsia can interfere with the blood supply to the placenta, impeding the proper delivery of oxygen and nourishment to the fetus, thus causing growth problems. Untreated preeclampsia can also progress into eclampsia—a condition in which blood pressure is so high it almost completely stops blood flow to the placenta and the danger of fetal death becomes quite high. Eclampsia can also be fatal to the mother or cause damage to her kidneys, liver, brain, and eyes. The hazards of preeclampsia and eclampsia, however, can be prevented with early detection and treatment.

The basic approach to treating mild preeclampsia is a) bed rest, lying on your side in particular, which enhances blood flow to the placenta. How much bed rest a day and for how many days will depend on how well your blood pressure responds to the treatment. In some cases, you can resume a limited schedule of activities after several days of bed rest, but sometimes you need to be confined to bed for the rest of the pregnancy (see pp. 129–31, under "Stress management," for more about bedrest in pregnancy); b) regular ultrasound examinations to make sure your baby is growing properly; c) regular blood pressure readings taken twice weekly by your doctor and daily by yourself; d) daily weight checks to monitor for any sudden rises; and e) a diet high in protein (ninety grams a day), which seems to help keep blood pressure regulated.

If these tactics are successful in controlling your blood pressure, there is usually no reason why you won't be able to continue your pregnancy and go into labor and deliver naturally. But if your symptoms don't stabilize or if your preeclampsia is moderate to severe, hospitalization and/or induced labor and early delivery may be necessary.

The "cure" for preeclampsia is delivery: once your baby is born, your blood pressure should go back to its prepregnancy levels. Also, as a rule, if you develop preeclampsia in your first pregnancy and develop it toward the end of the pregnancy, you're unlikely to have the problem again in future pregnancies.

ॐ *Your Diet*

MILK ALTERNATIVES

While drinking four eight-ounce glasses of milk everyday is the simplest way of making certain you get enough calcium (twelve hundred milligrams daily) during pregnancy, it is possible to get your calcium from other foods, too. The following foods provide approximately the same amount of calcium found in one glass of milk (three hundred milligrams):

8 ounces plain, flavored, or fruited yogurt
1 cup buttermilk
3-ounce tin of sardines with bones
1 ounce Swiss cheese
1½ ounces cheddar or American cheese
1 cup pudding
½ cup part-skin ricotta cheese
4 ounces canned salmon with bones

A combination of any two of the following foods provide the equivalent of a glass of milk:

8 ounces cottage cheese
2 tablespoons Parmesan cheese

6 ounces frozen yogurt
4 ounces canned shrimp
½ cup ice cream
1 ounce mozzarella cheese
1 cup oysters
4 ounces tofu
1 tablespoon blackstrap molasses

ê▲   *BUTTERMILK SMOOTHIE*   ê▲

Because of the "butter" in its name, buttermilk is mistakenly
believed to be rich in calories and fat. But buttermilk, which is
milk that has been fermented with bacteria to give it a distinct
thickness and tart taste, is not only butter-free, it is generally
quite low in fat (1½ percent fat) and calories (110 per cup).

The Smoothie provides three hundred milligrams of calcium,
the same amount of calcium you get from a glass of milk. It's a
great mid-afternoon snack, just about filling enough to tide
you over until dinnertime. You can easily substitute other fruits
(fresh or frozen strawberries work particularly well) or even
skip the fruit entirely, since the simple mix of buttermilk and
orange juice is quite good.

1 cup buttermilk
½ cup orange juice
½ nectarine or peach
½ banana
3 or 4 ice cubes
Combine all the ingredients in a blender and whirl until
    smooth.

ê▲ Your Workout

WALL EXERCISES TO PREVENT VARICOSE VEINS

When your leg muscles are strong, the extra weight of pregnancy
is less tiring to support. Also, limber, toned legs are ones that
have good circulation, and good blood flow to calf muscles may
help prevent varicose veins.

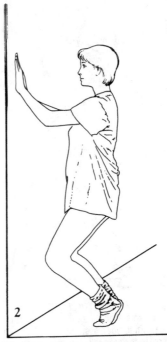

Wall Stretch for Front Thigh Muscles: 1. Stand with your feet together, an arm's length away from the wall. Place your hands flat on the wall. Rise up on your toes, and tighten your buttocks. 2. Slowly bend your knees, dropping down until you feel the stretch in the front of your thighs. Hold for five seconds. Rise up and repeat. To increase the stretch, let your bended knees part and hold to the count of five.

Varicose veins are encouraged by two factors during pregnancy: a) there is an increase in pressure in leg veins, caused by the increase in blood volume, and b) there is a decrease in the resistance in the walls of veins, caused by the extra progesterone which softens and relaxes vein walls. Although some women seem to be more predisposed to varicose veins than others, everyone can benefit from taking preventive measures. Besides doing the exercises illustrated above and on p. 106, it helps to avoid sitting with your legs crossed, to rotate your ankles frequently to promote good circulation, and to elevate your feet and legs whenever possible. Some women also find that wearing maternity support hose helps minimize achiness and swelling.

Wall Shift for Inner Thighs: 1. Stand with your feet flat on the floor, legs spread widely apart, arms a length away from the wall. Place your hands on the wall. 2. Bend your right knee, lifting your heel. Hold stretch to the count of ten. Repeat with left knee. You can increase the stretch by spreading your legs farther and/or bending deeper at the knee.

❧ *Your Feelings*

WHEN PREGNANCY GOES PUBLIC

In a sense, your pregnancy becomes public property once you begin to show. Everyone feels free to comment upon it. Passing acquaintances may stop and tell you what not to eat and drink; people you barely know may feel free to stroke your stomach; and practically everyone will want to offer you advice and opinions.

I can't count the number of people who approached me to offer their unsolicited predictions of my baby's sex (the nine out of ten who predicted a boy were wrong). The local greengrocer, dry cleaner, and UPS man all warned that I walked too fast for the baby's good. Complete strangers on the street called out comments about my size like "Any day now?" "Must be twins," and "That's going to be one big baby." (These comments started when I was only seven months pregnant and they made me feel very self-conscious about my weight gain, despite the fact that I knew it wasn't excessive. It did make me feel a little better, though, when I began to realize that these comments usually came from people who knew nothing about pregnancy and/or who had little contact with pregnant women.)

Family, friends and co-workers may also begin treating you differently as your pregnancy becomes more visible. Some people equate pregnancy with illness or a physical disability and so may tend to treat you as if you were frail and vulnerable (I found that older people in particular tended to do this). Friends who don't have children may avoid you or be slightly hostile because of underlying envy—of your fertility or simply of the circumstances of your life. Colleagues may unconsciously exclude you from professional discussions, making the assumption that all you want to talk about now is babies and pregnancy. Your burgeoning belly may even make some people nervous, since your sexuality has now become undeniable.

You're also likely to be surprised at how positive reactions can be. Many of my childless friends grew genuinely curious about my pregnancy as my size increased. They really wanted to hear all the details, to find out what it was really like.

A longtime college friend always went out of his way to make me feel good, by insisting that he found pregnant women sexy. I also found that men and women who had recently had a child invariably approached me with enthusiasm and aimed to offer emotional support. Mothers of all ages asked me how far along I was, then warmly wished me luck. And true to the cliché, people really did offer me their seat on both buses and subways.

The private side of going public. Just as the reaction of others to the visibility of your pregnancy is complicated and varied, so may be your own reaction to it. At first, you may be happy when you start to show; many women find that they are relieved that people will no longer think they are just "fat."

It's during the second trimester that you're likely to have the most positive feelings about your pregnant appearance.

It's easy in the middle months to feel proud of the fact that you're sharing your body with another being, since your belly is just big enough to confirm the reality of your pregnancy but not so big that you feel unattractive or clumsy. Since you don't feel unwieldy yet, looking pregnant may make you feel more "womanly"; it may even make you secretly feel somehow more powerful and fulfilled than nonpregnant women. But since being pregnant has such obvious sexual implications, you may also discover that you feel slightly embarrassed around certain people (such as your boss or father, for instance).

Especially as the third trimester unfolds, a positive body image can get increasingly harder to maintain. The bigger you get, the easier it is to feel that you've somehow lost control over your body.

I not only began to feel conspicuous and awkward, I found I became increasingly preoccupied with the permanent changes pregnancy might make on my body. I mostly worried that I would never be thin again (my worries were unfounded as it turned out—I was back to my prepregnancy weight within three months postpartum). It's also common to worry about your vagina stretching permanently, changes in your skin tone, venous changes, stretch marks, and/or the appearance of your breasts. These anxieties are likely to be most intense during the last weeks of pregnancy when your size is the most overpowering and when concerns about the upcoming labor and delivery can make you particularly vulnerable.

Participating in childbirth education classes (see pp. 131–33) is probably the best way to combat negative body image in the last trimester. A class gives you the chance to compare your body with those of other pregnant women; seeing that you're not the only one who looks and feels like a "watermelon," "blimp," or "elephant" can be strangely reassuring.

Most classes also teach you about the anatomy and physiology of pregnancy, and incorporate relaxation techniques that encourage you to work with your body in tandem with your partner. This can help you feel more in command of your body and so help you to accept your body changes. Most childbirth classes include a session on postpartum recovery, too, which can give you faith that your body will, in fact, revert back to its prepregnant shape.

ཉ Your Life-Style

TRAVELING

If your pregnancy isn't considered high risk, you should be able to travel up until your thirty-sixth week. After that, many airlines won't let you fly (check with your travel agent or ticketing agent for specific regulations regarding the airline you'll be using). And, you might want to keep car, bus, and rail trips short in the last month because of the chance of early labor.

If your pregnancy is high risk (you have a history of bleeding, hypertension, or are severely anemic, for example) you should consult your doctor before traveling. He or she may discourage you from taking long trips in the last trimester.

For the most part, if you are traveling in the U.S., you don't need to take any special precautions just because you're pregnant. However, if you are contemplating travel to a foreign country, being pregnant does demand some special consideration. The American College of Obstetricians and Gynecologists (ACOG) does not recommend travel to countries that require immunization, since most vaccines pose potential risks to the fetus. ACOG offers these additional guidelines for travel to foreign countries:

• Bring a copy of your prenatal medical record with you. In the off-chance that an emergency arises, it may be easier for a foreign doctor to understand a written medical record rather than a verbal explanation.

• Carry a good foreign-language dictionary with you, one that includes basic medical terms that apply to pregnancy. Again, in the unlikely event that you need medical assistance, your knowing certain key words can make communication faster and easier.

• Find out where the nearest medical facility is in each place you visit. A phone call or stop at the nearest U.S. embassy can provide you with this information. Or, the International Association for Medical Assistance to Travelers can provide you with a list of English-speaking doctors and member hospitals abroad. You can write IAMAT at 417 Center Street, Lewiston, NY 14092 or call (716) 754-4883.

• Don't drink the tap water. Drink only bottled water.

• Avoid fresh fruit and vegetables if the country you are visiting has a reputation for making foreigners ill. For instance, many Americans become sick when they eat fresh produce in Mexico, since their digestive systems are not accustomed to the microorganisms found on local produce. Few U. S. citizens, on the other hand, seem to run into trouble in France or Italy. Your travel agent should be able to help you with this kind of information.

• Don't eat raw or undercooked meat, since it may contain an organism that can cause toxoplasmosis (see pp. 38–39).

• Make sure the milk you drink is pasteurized, (and the cheese you eat is made from pasteurized milk), since some countries don't require pasteurization.

7

MONTH SIX

(22½ to 27 WEEKS)

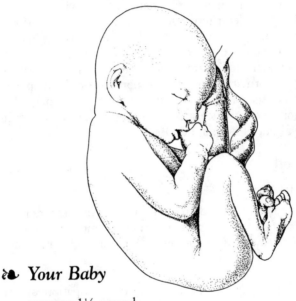

≥ *Your Baby*

WEIGHT: 1½ pounds
LENGTH: 11 to 14 inches

The fetus's ears now function. But what does it hear? Your heart beating, your stomach rumbling, and all the other noises made by your internal workings. It's also likely that the fetus can hear external sounds; that is, noises outside the womb.

Several studies indicate that the fetus, in utero, can be startled by loud, sudden noises. Research also suggests that newborns recognize their mothers' voices at birth and may even remember music they heard repetitively while in the womb. In a recent European experiment, the theme song of a popular soap opera was played for a group of four- and five-day-old infants. The babies whose mothers regularly watched the soap during pregnancy became noticeably calm, attentive, and quiet. In contrast, the babies whose mothers didn't watch the show generally didn't react or change their behavior (they kept crying, for instance) in response to the tune.

By the end of this month, the fetus opens and closes his or her eyes, starts thumb-sucking, and reaches a major milestone: with intensive care, he or she now has a chance of surviving if born. Before this time, the fetal lungs are too immature to function, but at approximately twenty-four weeks, the fetus begins to manufacture surfactant, a protein that coats the lining of the lungs, enabling them to inflate and deflate properly. Although almost all babies born at the end of this month need the help of a mechanical ventilator to breathe, the fact that they have developed the ability to produce surfactant gives them a chance not only of survival but of normal development.

?● Your Body

COMMON SIDE EFFECTS OF LATE PREGNANCY

Pregnancy is the cause, but delivery isn't the only treatment for the following complaints: in many cases, symptoms may be relieved or even avoided altogether if you eat right and keep moderately active.

Constipation. You may be more prone to constipation during pregnancy for two reasons: the hormone progesterone relaxes the bowel somewhat, making it slower to eliminate stools; and the enlarging uterus compresses the bowel.

The best and safest way to prevent, as well as remedy, constipation is to eat a diet that's high in fiber (see "Natural Constipation Remedies," pp. 120–21) and to drink generous amounts of liquids every day. This ensures that stools are soft and easy to pass. Also, getting a moderate amount of exercise daily helps stimulate your bowels to keep wastes passing through.

If your constipation is severe, there are some over-the-counter laxatives that are thought to be safe for use during pregnancy. But you should check with your obstetrician before using them and they should never be used as a substitute for the diet and exercise tactics already mentioned. Laxatives are a "last-resort" remedy, since the more regularly you rely on a laxative, the lazier your bowel becomes and, thus, the more dependent on them you become. Also, mineral oil is not recommended for use during pregnancy since it can interfere with the absorption of the fat-soluble vitamins A, D and E.

Hemorrhoids. These are enlarged, swollen veins around the rectum and anus. External hemorrhoids develop on the outside of the anal canal. These round, purplish swellings (which can be anywhere from pea- to grape-sized) may feel tender, itchy, and painful. Internal hemorrhoids, which are located inside the rectum, usually bleed after a bowel movement but don't usually cause pain.

As the uterus enlarges, it exerts pressure on the anorectal veins. This factor in itself, though, doesn't usually cause hemorrhoids. It's when anorectal veins get further stressed by forceful straining (i.e., pushing to pass stools when you're constipated) that hemorrhoids often develop.

As with constipation, the best approach to hemorrhoids is a preventive one. Eating lots of fibery foods, drinking plenty of liquids, and exercising moderately helps ensure that hemorrhoids never surface in the first place. If they do develop, a good diet keeps discomfort to a minimum, plus helps them disappear quickly.

There are several home remedies that help ease the pain and itching of hemorrhoids. First, after a bowel movement, avoid wiping vigorously, which irritates swollen tissues. Instead, clean the area gently with water, then pat it dry or use treated "wipes" (such as Preparation H medicated cleansing pads or Tucks), which have a coating that also temporarily soothes and cools. Hot and cold temperatures also provide relief: soaking in a warm tub for fifteen minutes twice a day and/or applying an ice pack to the anal region helps reduce swelling and so lessens pain.

Most over-the-counter ointments and suppositories marketed to treat hemorrhoids are thought to be safe for use during pregnancy (as always, check with your doctor first). But like laxatives, these can "backfire" if overused, making your hemorrhoids even more swollen than when you started. Most pregnancy-related hemorrhoids, including the ones that surface after labor and delivery as a result of pushing, can be expected to disappear in a month or two with home care. Persistently painful hemorrhoids can usually be quickly and easily removed in an office or day-surgery procedure.

Heartburn. Often called acid indigestion, this burning sensation felt in your throat and esophagus is caused by the backing up of the stomach contents. This spilling back is more likely to occur during pregnancy because the enlarging uterus puts pressure on the stomach as well as pushes it up; in addition, progesterone causes the stomach "valve" that stops gastric reflux to relax somewhat. For heartburn relief tactics, see pp. 134–35.

Shortness of breath (dyspnea). In the last months of pregnancy, the uterus can crowd the diaphragm, making you short-winded. Some women find breathing particularly difficult at night, when they are trying to sleep. When that's the case, propping your head and shoulders up, on two pillows, often helps. In the last weeks of pregnancy, the baby moves away from the diaphragm and down toward the pelvis, which means breathing usually returns to normal.

Swollen legs and feet. Swelling in the legs, ankles, and feet is quite common in the last months of pregnancy. What happens is that the growing uterus constricts major veins that lead from the heart to the legs, and while blood has no problem flowing down to the legs, it has a hard time pumping back up, against the force of gravity and through constricted veins to the heart. The result is fluid accumulates faster in your lower extremities than it is removed.

Not illogically, putting your feet up is the best way to increase venous return to the heart and to relieve swelling, which tends to be most pronounced at the end of the day and/or after long periods of standing. Sleeping on your left side, which takes the pressure off the main vein (the vena cava) that's responsible for transporting blood from the lower body back to the heart, helps keep swelling from progressively worsening. Maternity support hose can help improve circulation and thus minimize swelling (although these hose can sometimes be uncomfortable). It also helps to keep your legs elevated whenever possible, to change positions frequently when sitting, to avoid long periods of standing, and to choose socks without tight elastic tops.

Some puffiness is normal, but there is a point at which swelling can signal a problem. If your face, eyes, and hands become puffy, if you gain more than two pounds a week, and/or if the swelling in your feet and legs isn't relieved by a forty-five minute period of elevation, you should see your doctor right away, since these things could be symptoms of pregnancy-induced hypertension (see pp. 101–03).

Calluses, corns, and blisters. Even if you don't really notice the difference, your shoes may begin to fit somewhat differently as a result of your weight gain. This change in fit can create friction, which in turn can lead to the formation of calluses (tough layers of dead skin, usually on the heels and balls of the feet), corns (thick, hard plugs of dead skin on the toes or soles), and/or blisters (tender, swollen areas, usually with clear fluid underneath). Later in pregnancy, some women find that their feet change so much that they have to buy new shoes, up to one full size larger.

If your calluses and/or corns aren't painful and their appearance doesn't bother you, there's no medical reason to remove them. But if you want to be rid of them, you can self-treat using a pumice stone (which you can usually buy in drugstores). Each day after showering, use the stone to slough off a layer of dead skin, being careful not to remove too much at one time (which can leave an area raw and tender). If your corns or calluses are painful (which they can be when they become so thick as to push against the bones of your feet), you should consult a podiatrist, who can safely remove them in one office visit.

To treat a blister, apply an antiseptic gel or cream, then place a bandage over it. Try to resist popping it, since it will heal faster and will be less prone to infection if it is allowed to burst on its own.

Round ligament pain. The round ligaments support the uterus; they're right under your belly, in your groin region. When these supportive structures get overstretched, the pain, which is usually felt on one side and lessens when you lie down on the side in which you feel the pain, can be deep and gripping. Because the pain usually feels quite serious, most women naturally contact their doctors, who can then definitively rule out premature labor, appendicitis, or other disorders as the cause. In general, round ligament pain goes away on its own, within twenty-four to forty-eight hours.

Upper abdominal pain. Some women experience extreme pain (which they describe as charley horse–esque or like "internal bruising") across their upper abdomen. This is probably a result of the liver being pushed and crowded by the expanding uterus and fetus (see illustration, p. 14). The pain can be excruciating, especially when your baby lands a kick or punch in the upper abdominal region. Unfortunately, there is not much you can do to relieve this pain (which may get worse when you lie down). However, you may be able to take some small comfort from the fact that what you are feeling is normal and not a sign of any serious problem.

❧   COLOSTRUM AND CONTRACTIONS   ❧

• Some women (but not all) leak a little *colostrum* during the last months of pregnancy. Colostrum is the thin, sticky, amber-colored pre-milk that flows during the first two to three days postpartum (after that, your milk comes in). It not only provides perfect nutrition for your baby's first days of life, it has a unique array of antibodies that protect your newborn from disease.

• Everyone experiences *Braxton-Hicks contractions* in the last months of pregnancy, although you might not be aware of them. That's because these vague, uncoordinated tightenings of the uterus—which seem to "tune up" the uterus to get ready for the real labor—are usually painless and so can be easy to overlook.

❧ *Your Doctor Appointment*

YOUR GLUCOSE TOLERANCE TEST
FOR GESTATIONAL DIABETES

This month your doctor is likely to test you for gestational diabetes, a form of temporary diabetes that surfaces (usually without producing any symptoms) between the twenty-fourth and twenty-eighth week of pregnancy. Although gestational diabetes probably affects less than 5 percent of all pregnant women, most major health organizations recommend all expectant women be screened for it since, if left untreated, it can cause serious problems for both mother and baby.

Gestational diabetes is thought to be triggered by the hormonal changes of pregnancy. At about this time (the sixth month) the placenta and the mother's body produce hormones that increase blood-sugar (glucose) levels so as to provide ample nourishment for the fast-growing fetus. Normally, the pancreas responds to this rise in blood sugar by producing more insulin, the substance that processes blood sugar so cells can use it for energy. But in some pregnant women, the pancreas doesn't produce the extra insulin needed to process blood sugar, so an excess of sugar builds up in the mother's blood and produces the condition known as gestational diabetes.

Diagnosing gestational diabetes early, then controlling blood-sugar levels properly, is crucial to the health of both mother and baby. Untreated, gestational diabetes poses these risks:

• High birth weight (macrosomia). When the mother's pancreas fails to produce enough insulin, the fetus's pancreas kicks in and manufactures it; in that way the fetus protects itself from getting an excess of glucose. But since insulin acts as a growth hormone in the fetus, the result can be an over-big baby (over ten pounds). Oversized babies are difficult and sometimes dangerous to deliver vaginally, and so are frequently delivered by cesarean section.

• Low blood sugar. As already mentioned, the baby, in utero, produces extra insulin so it can process the high levels of glucose it receives from its mother. Unfortunately, after birth, the baby may keep producing this extra insulin, even though there's less glucose to process. As a consequence, the baby may overprocess its own blood sugar and actually develop low blood sugar, which, if prolonged, can lead to brain damage.

• Respiratory Distress Syndrome (RDS). When high maternal blood sugar goes uncontrolled, a baby's nervous system, heart, and lungs may be temporarily impaired, making breathing difficult at first.

• Stillbirth. It's not well understood why, but when untreated, diabetes is associated with a higher risk of fetal death.

Who's at risk. Any expectant woman can develop gestational diabetes, although women who begin pregnancy overweight; have a family history of diabetes; have had the disorder in previous pregnancies; have delivered babies over ten pounds; or have had a previous stillbirth are at higher risk. Being over thirty years old also puts you at a slightly higher risk, since susceptibility rises with age.

The symptoms of gestational diabetes—increased hunger, thirst, need to urinate, and/or feelings of weakness—can be hard to distinguish from the normal side effects of pregnancy. What's more, many women feel no signs at all. The first indication they get that there's a problem is when their doctor notifies them that their glucose tolerance test is positive.

The glucose tolerance test is simple to take: you drink a big glass of sugary-tasting glucose solution, wait an hour, then have a blood test. The results are usually ready in twenty-four hours; if you test positive, you then need to take a longer (three-hour) test to definitively confirm the first test's readings.

Treatment. It's only in rare cases that gestational diabetes must be treated with insulin injections; in most cases, a carefully controlled diet is enough to prevent swings in blood-glucose levels. Usually this diet stresses protein and complex carbohydrates, excludes any concentrated sweets, and is structured so that meals and snacks are eaten throughout the day, every few hours, to keep blood-sugar levels on an even keel.

In addition, you may need to monitor your blood-sugar levels daily at home. At-home blood-glucose tests rely on a simple device that pricks your finger in a relatively painless, quick fashion; you then test this blood sample using a special meter or paper strips.

Delivery and beyond. When gestational diabetes is well controlled, delivery and labor have no greater risk of being complicated than in a normal pregnancy. But if the diabetes has been difficult to control, the baby may become too large or be at risk in other ways, and so early delivery (via induced labor or cesarean section) may be necessary.

After delivery, the blood-sugar levels of most women return to normal within a few weeks. But about 50 percent of all women who experience gestational diabetes go on to develop permanent diabetes within ten years. For this reason, yearly testing is recommended for all women who have experienced gestational diabetes. These women should also carefully watch their diet and weight, since keeping healthy can help delay the onset and reduce the severity of permanent diabetes or even prevent it from surfacing.

STREP B ALERT

Between the twenty-sixth and twenty-eighth week of pregnancy, more and more doctors now routinely screen for the bacteria strep B (group B streptococcus). This bacteria is normally symptomless and harmless in adults. However, if transmitted at delivery to a newborn, it is potentially fatal. Although only 2 percent of all strep B–infected babies actually get sick, once symptoms appear, they can cause permanent brain damage or death within hours (symptoms, which usually surface in the first week of life, are deceptively similar to that of a common cold: sleepiness, fussiness, fever, and breathing difficulty). So ask your doctor about being tested (all it takes is a culture, obtained with a simple vaginal swab). If you test positive, your pregnancy will be monitored closely and you may need to be treated with antibiotics at delivery.

ﻬ Your Diet

NATURAL CONSTIPATION REMEDIES

There are lots of healthful reasons to include fiber in your diet. It helps keep cholesterol levels down, blood-sugar levels even, and colon cancer risks low. But during pregnancy, when intestinal action often slows due to the rise of progesterone and the pressing of the enlarging uterus on the bowel, the particular importance of fiber is that it helps keep you "regular." This, in turn, helps ensure that you don't need to depend on laxatives. (Repeated laxative use cannot only interfere with the absorption of various vitamins and minerals, it can cause your bowel muscles to become habitually lazy, leading to chronic constipation.)

Fiber passes through your gastrointestinal tract undigested; it contributes to regularity by absorbing water as it passes through your system, thus making your stools bulky, soft, and easy to pass. Whole grains, beans, vegetables, and fruits all contain fiber. Some of these are better bulking agents than others, but you shouldn't overemphasize any one fiber source. Instead, it's important to eat a wide variety of fiber-rich foods to be sure you not only avoid constipation but also get the wide variety of vitamins and minerals you need during pregnancy.

The pregnancy diet outlined on pp. 23–27 includes lots of fibery foods; if you follow it, constipation is not likely to become a problem. It's especially important to stick to the "drink six to eight glasses of water daily" rule, since without adequate liquid to soak up, fiber will get "stuck" and could actually be constipating.

But if, despite your best efforts, you find you're irregular, you can combat it with the following traditional, natural remedies. These remedies are not therapeutic golden bullets that will relieve constipation if your diet is unhealthy. They can complement a healthful diet, however, supplementing it when your digestive system needs a little coaxing along during pregnancy.

Prunes. Drinking a glass of prune juice in the morning, then eating four to six stewed prunes in the evening before going to bed is a time-honored way to keep regular.

Bran. Eating a bowl of high-fiber cereal, such as All-Bran, 100% Bran or Bran Buds, or adding one tablespoon of raw bran to yogurt or other types of breakfast cereal can help ensure you have a daily bowel movement. Beware of bran muffins, though, since many commercially baked varieties are high in sugar, fat, and caramel coloring (to make them look "healthy") and are not particularly rich in bran fiber.

Raw carrots. Most vegetables are good sources of fiber, but carrots are one of the best. Eating one or two daily may help keep your digestive workings on track, as well as supply you with healthy amounts of vitamin A and potassium.

Figs. Like prunes, figs are a folk-medicine laxative, and they are, in fact, quite high in fiber. Fresh figs are delicious if you can find them, but dried figs are equally fiber-rich.

Molasses. A teaspoon of molasses a day is a home cure for constipation. It may or may not be effective; it's harmless, though, if you're inclined to give it a try.

≈● Your Workout

THE GROWING PAIN

There are two body changes that make you more prone to backaches when you're pregnant: the normally rock-stable joints of your pelvis soften, giving your spine less support, and the added weight of your abdomen can pull you forward, causing your back to sway and strain.

The best way to overcome back pain is to avoid it in the first place. Practice good posture: When standing, place your feet a shoulder width apart, bearing your weight equally on each foot. Your shoulders should be back, not rigid, but comfortable, and your belly should be pulled in. Wear low-heeled, well-supported shoes, and never lift heavy loads by bending at your waist (bend at the knees instead, then lift weight slowly using your arm muscles). Also, since the pressure on the lower spine is inten-

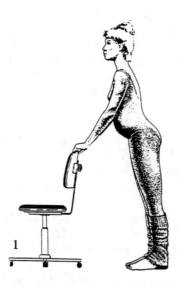

Pelvic rock: 1. Stand about two feet away from the back of a chair, bend slightly forward from your hips, and place your hands on a chair back, keeping your elbows straight.

sified when you sit for long periods, it helps to get up, stretch, and move around frequently.

In addition, a time-honored pregnancy exercise, "the pelvic rock," helps relieve backaches by strengthening your abdominal muscles (which provide crucial support to your spine) and by increasing the overall flexibility of your lower back. The illustration above shows how to do the exercise.

❧ *Your Feelings*

PREGNANT WITH A SECOND CHILD

There's one thought that crosses the minds of most parents expecting a second child: "I'm afraid I won't be able to love my second child as much as I love my first." Happily, the almost universal discovery postpartum is that you can and do love the second as much. Perhaps the process of attachment may be different (it seems to be slower for second-time fathers in par-

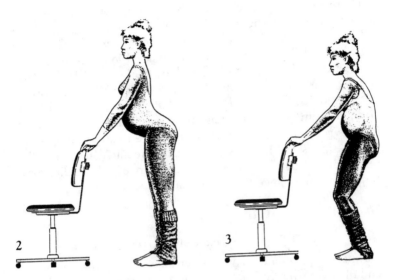

2. Gently thrust hips backward so you have a "sway back." 3. Bend your knees slightly and begin rotating your hips forward and back, being sure to tighten your abdominal muscles and tuck your buttocks in as you do it. Repeat ten times. Doing this exercise twenty to twenty-five times throughout the day will help keep your back limber and pain-free.

ticular), and you may love the second differently—but differently doesn't mean not equally or without equal strength.

The other major concern most second-time parents-to-be have centers on the issue of sibling rivalry. Although a great deal has been written on this subject, three incontrovertible facts seem to rise from the collective literature:

1. Your firstborn can no longer be your one and only.

2. Your second child can never be treated exactly as your first.

3. It's impossible to shield your children completely from sibling rivalry.

But these facts are not entirely negative. For instance, while it's true that your firstborn may have to learn to share you, in doing so he or she will gain someone to share memories and experiences with throughout the rest of his or her life. And while a second child can never receive as much undivided attention as your first did, a second reaps immeasurable benefits from the fact that you are experienced this time around.

There are an array of children's books designed to help prepare an older child for the arrival of a new brother or sister. The following titles are for children under four years old: *The New Baby* by Fred Rogers (New York: Putnam, 1985), *Hello Baby* by Charlotte Doyle (New York: Random House, 1989), *The New Baby at Your House* by Joanna Cole (New York: William Morrow, 1985) and *101 Things to Do with a Baby* by Jan Ormerod (New York: Penguin, 1986). In addition, most general childcare guides include good sections on how to minimize rivalry (see pp. 180–81 for suggestions). In essence, what's required most of all is sensitivity, empathy, and a simple acceptance of the reality that a new baby will change the present family equilibrium.

❧ *Your Life-Style*

THE BARE-BONES BABY BUYING LIST

During my pregnancy, I was never able to read through to the end of any of the lists of "layette and nursery needs" that I often came across in baby magazines. Those lists not only tended to be dauntingly long, they almost always included things, such as safety gates, potty seats, and walking shoes, that were needs too far into the future for me to think about then, at pre-birth.

Now that I've had a baby, I also know that much of the stuff those lists included is unnecessary. For instance, you don't need six crib sheets (unless you only do laundry once a month), you don't need baby oil (what's the point when the baby's skin is already so soft?), and you probably don't need waterproof pants or safety pins even if you use cloth diapers (you'll probably want to use fabric diaper covers instead).

So here's a skeletal list of what you'll need within the first month, remembering that it's not as if you can't go shopping to fill in any gaps after the baby is born.

Clothing. If you do laundry every other day, you can probably get away with the lower amount; if you only do laundry twice a week, you need the higher amount.

- undershirts (three to five)
- sleepers (two to four)

- one-piece coveralls (three to five) (ones that snap or zipper up the front make diaper-changing easy; if the weather is cool, buy these with built-in feet since it can be impossible to keep socks on a baby)
- hat (one either to shield the baby from sun or keep him or her warm)
- snowsuit, if weather demands it
- bath towels (two to four)

Diapers

- Disposables: you'll need about two 66-count bags of small-sized diapers per week
- Diaper service: you need approximately one hundred diapers delivered, plus four to five diaper covers (I found Diaperaps to be the most inexpensive covers, and the easiest to use and care for. Call 1-800-251-4321)
- Home-laundered diapers: you'll need three to four dozen if you do laundry every other day, plus four to five diaper covers

Pharmacy/grocery items

- digital thermometer
- nail scissors
- diaper rash ointment
- baby shampoo
- baby soap
- cotton swabs
- soft paper towels and tissues (I use these with plain water instead of the premoistened towelettes, which often contain chemicals and fragrances)
- formula, if bottle-feeding
- baby laundry detergent

Feeding supplies

- If breast-feeding: one box of nursing pads to protect clothes from leaks; two nursing bras

• If bottle-feeding: disposable nurser kit or four four-ounce bottles

Bedding

• crib sheets (three are enough)
• one crib underpad
• blankets (how many depends on the climate, but almost everyone will need at least two lightweight cotton thermal blankets and one heavier-weight wool one)

The bigger-ticket baby equipment

• crib (although in the first weeks, a bassinet or Moses basket with padding will suffice for the baby's bed)
• car seat
• stroller
• front carrier
• changing table (if you have ample counter space in your bathroom, you may not need this. Also, you may not need a baby bathtub—a towel or sponge lining the bottom of the sink usually suffices in the first weeks)

The two free guides below will provide you with detailed information on what safety features to look for in this nursery equipment; these guides also give you information on other things, like bassinets, toy chests, pacifiers, etc.

"The Safe Nursery"
Write: U.S. Consumer Product Safety Commission, Washington, DC 20207

"The Family Shopping Guide"
Write: American Academy of Pediatrics, 141 Northwest Point Blvd., Elk Grove Village, IL 60007; send a stamped, self-addressed envelope.

8

MONTH SEVEN

(27 TO 31½ WEEKS)

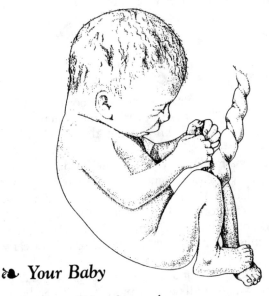

⫸ *Your Baby*

WEIGHT: 2½ to 3 pounds
LENGTH: 14 to 17 inches

During these weeks, the fetal central nervous system becomes capable of controlling body temperature, a function that greatly increases the chances of survival if the baby is born now. In fact, each day the fetus spends growing and gaining weight inside the womb serves to dramatically increase its chances of surviving and thriving outside of it. That's why doctors aggressively try to stop or stall premature labor, even if just for a few days, whenever possible.

The fetus may get the hiccups now; you may feel them as rhythmic little jolts or jerks. The tendency to hiccup continues after birth as well (but newborns don't seem bothered by their hiccuping, which starts for no apparent reason and stops by itself).

Head hair starts to grow. If, that is, your baby is destined to be born with any: some babies arrive with thick, luxurious locks, while others are born with barely a follicle. The color of the hair that is growing isn't necessarily permanent, though. When babies are about four months old, new hair, often of a new color, replaces the old.

❧ *Your Body*

RECOGNIZING THE SIGNS OF PRETERM LABOR

As many as 40 percent of all premature babies are born to women who were thought to be at "low risk" for early labor, which is why every pregnant woman needs to know what the symptoms of premature labor are.

The initial symptoms rarely hit you over the head. Not only can they be vague, they're easy to ignore since you're not really expecting to go into labor. At term, for example, you're likely to be hypervigilant, looking for the slightest sign of labor, whereas at thirty-one weeks you simply aren't primed to pay much attention to the mild aches and pains that are characteristic of early labor.

Listed below are the signs that are suggestive of preterm labor. If you feel any of them, you're likely to think, "Oh, it's probably nothing." The chances are good that you're right (since 85 to 95 percent of all births *aren't* premature), but a prompt call to your doctor is warranted, since the earlier preterm labor is diagnosed, the greater the chance it can be successfully delayed (delaying delivery, even if it's only for one day, can, in some cases, make a huge difference in a "preemie's" chance for survival).

Symptoms of Preterm Labor

- Achiness in the lower back region
- Mild pelvic soreness or cramps (akin to what you might feel before a period)

- Painless tightenings and/or pressure in your lower abdomen
- Noticeably more frequent bowel movements and/or diarrhea
- Markedly increased vaginal discharge and/or discharge that's mucusy, watery, or blood-tinged
- Contractions, especially ones that occur with any kind of regularity (every twenty minutes for instance) and/or last for more than thirty seconds

When preterm contractions are detected, drug therapy is usually begun quickly (the possible cause is investigated, too, since preterm contractions are sometimes triggered by dehydration, a fever, a cervical infection, or a urinary tract infection). Drugs to stop labor work by relaxing the uterine muscles and are generally administered intravenously at first, which means you must stay in a hospital during treatment. Once labor stops, you're given medication orally; if, with the oral doses, the uterus continues to remain relaxed, doses are gradually lowered until medication is stopped completely.

Labor-stopping drugs don't seem to have any long-term effects on the fetus. Two seemingly harmless short-term effects include a temporary increase in fetal heart rate and a decrease in blood sugar. For the mother-to-be, though, these drugs can induce heart palpitations as well as feelings of nervousness and restlessness—side effects that, unfortunately, can make an already stressful situation even worse.

Most post-hospitalization prescriptions include the following elements:

1. *Rest.* Depending on your due date and condition, you may be instructed to stay in bed constantly or only instructed to lie down on your left side for one hour twice a day.

2. *Fluid.* Eight to ten cups a day is prescribed.

3. *Limited sexual activity.* You may be told to stop having intercourse; nipple stimulation should be avoided.

5. *Monitoring.* You may be instructed to wear an electronic fetal monitor, which is worn like a belt, one hour twice a day, to detect any increases in uterine activity.

6. *Stress management.* While a prescription of extended bed rest may sound inviting in the abstract, it can be extremely isolating, depressing, and frustrating in reality. Not only are most

women overcome by worries about their baby's health, they feel guilty about having to depend on their partner for everything, feel pressured by the demands of older children, and are worried about money not being earned or being lost to hospital bills.

Knowing all this, some physicians will put you in touch with other pregnant women also confined to bed or will refer you to a counselor you can turn to for help in coping with the situation. You can also contact the "Confinement Line," a free telephone support network staffed by volunteers who were once confined to bed themselves during pregnancy. The telephone number is 703-941-7183, or you can write the Confinement Line (which also publishes a newsletter), c/o The Childbirth Education Association, P.O. Box 1609, Springfield, VA 22151.

In addition, you may want to get the pamphlet "Bedrest in Pregnancy." This mini-survival guide was written by Susan Green Hoffman, a certified nurse-midwife who had to spend nine weeks in bed during her third pregnancy. For a copy send $.50

ఎ ARE YOU AT SPECIAL RISK FOR PREMATURE LABOR? ఎ

The factors below have all been shown to correlate with an increased risk of premature labor. If any of these factors apply to you, you'll want to be especially attentive to the signs of the onset of labor:

- Carrying twins, triplets, quadruplets, etc.
- Having an infection
- Being a smoker (especially if you smoke more than ten cigarettes a day)
- DES exposure
- Previous preterm labor and/or delivery
- Uterine fibroids
- Poor weight gain
- Abdominal surgery during pregnancy
- Abnormally shaped uterus
- Incompetent cervix
- Second- or third-trimester bleeding

and a self-addressed, stamped envelope to Pennypress Inc., 1100 23rd Avenue East, Seattle, WA 98112. Also available is *Pregnancy Bedrest: A Guidebook for the Pregnant Woman and Her Family* by Susan H. Johnston and Deborah A. Kraut. For a copy send a check for $10 to Pregnancy Bedrest, P.O. Box 7304, McLean, VA 22106-7304.

A preemie's prospects. What if labor and delivery can't be delayed? Today, the majority of premature babies do very well, suffering few, if any, long-term health effects. Still, many preemies require long hospitalizations, an experience that can be very difficult and frightening for new parents. Most of the baby-care books listed on pp. 180–81 devote a special section to premature babies. In addition, there's *The Premature Baby Book* by Helen Harrison and Ann Kositsky (New York: St. Martin's Press, 1983) and *Parenting Your Premature Baby* by Janine Jason (New York: Doubleday, 1990).

๛ *Your Doctor Appointment*

CHILDBIRTH EDUCATION CLASSES

By now, your caregiver has probably suggested you take a prepared childbirth course and has recommended a particular program, too.* Most classes are held at hospitals or maternity centers, and consist of six two-hour weekly sessions.

The chief purpose of childbirth preparation is to give you a basic education as to what to expect during labor and delivery. The underlying philosophy is that knowledge is power. The more you know, the less likely it is that you will be gripped by uncontrollable panic and fear—feelings that may not only magnify your pain but can even interfere with the progress of labor. Classes

---

*In the rare event that your caregiver has not recommended, or does not recommend prepared childbirth, you'll want to consider selecting a course on your own. Almost every community has at least one program; look in the Yellow Pages under Childbirth Education or Social Service Organizations or contact the maternity wards of local hospitals. About the only circumstance in which preparation might not be of benefit is if you are scheduled for a pre-labor cesarean birth.

also teach you relaxation and breathing techniques to help you cope with the pain of labor; they serve to educate your coach (usually your husband) as to his role, too.

There are several reasons why books (including this one) and/ or instructional videos can't really substitute for taking a live class. For starters, only a flesh-and-blood instructor can respond to your specific, personal questions or show you why your breathing technique is not as effective as it could be during practice sessions. Without the classroom setting and schedule, it also could be easy to "put off" educating yourself. Attending a class, in other words, ensures that you don't skip or skim over material you'd rather not deal with (but might have to). Finally, a class offers you the chance to be with other couples who are going through the same experience (I found it reassuring to simply see other women in the same stage of pregnancy that I was in). In fact, a strong bond of camaraderie very often emerges between class members as couples air their concerns, exchange pregnancy stories, and are generally emotionally supportive of each other.

The basic class ingredient list. Courses sponsored by a hospital or maternity center will include a tour of the labor/delivery rooms as well as a review of the maternity unit policies and procedures. In addition, almost all childbirth classes cover these eight topics:

1. Anatomy and physiology review—i.e., the basics of how the female body adapts for childbearing. Even if you are familiar with a lot of this information, it may be eye-opening for your coach

2. Pregnancy health issues—a discussion of common discomforts, nutritional needs, exercise guidelines, etc. Again, this information may not be new to you, but could be instructional for your coach

3. The laboring process—a detailed stage-by-stage description of what to expect during labor

4. Controlled relaxation and breathing exercises—techniques to help you stay in control and cope with pain

5. Medication and analgesia options—a complete description of painkilling choices, with a look at their side effects

6. Delivery—descriptions of what happens during just about every type of delivery (i.e., a normal vaginal delivery, forceps delivery, breech delivery, etc.) and what to expect if you need a cesarean section

7. Newborn care—how to change a diaper, breast- or bottle-feed, bathe the baby, and so on

8. The postpartum experience—information on the physical changes a new mother experiences, plus a look at some of the emotional aftereffects of having a baby

If it works, it's right. The best known methods of childbirth preparation are the Lamaze, Bradley, and Read methods. The similarities among these methods are greater than their differences, since each aims for the same thing: to help you cooperate with the normal process of labor so you can remain in control of yourself and actively participate in the birth of your baby. What's more, most childbirth educators today don't strictly adhere to any one school of thought; instead, they freely borrow a little from each method.

As a consumer, the most important thing to remember is that there is no one single "right" approach. For instance, my childbirth class instructor suggested that we keep our eyes open and focus on a favorite picture during labor as a way to distract us from contraction pain (a classic Lamaze technique). Yet I knew that, personally, I would be much more able to cope with pain if I closed my eyes, concentrated, and focused "inward." In other words, if there is something that somehow doesn't match your inclination or beliefs, talk with your instructor about alternative ideas. You might also want to read *Giving Birth: How It Really Feels* by Sheila Kitzinger (New York: Noonday Press, 1989), in which thirty women recount their birth experiences. Much more than reading about subtle philosophical differences in childbirth preparation methods, which I found far too abstract to be useful, I found that the ideas and insight I gained from reading firsthand accounts, in which women described what they felt and what they found helpful during labor, were an excellent supplement to the skills I learned in my childbirth class.

ﻬ   *CHILDREN IN THE DELIVERY ROOM*   ﻬ

Dads-to-be in the delivery room are by now standard fare, and most learn how to be good coaches in childbirth preparation classes. But having a child attend a birth is still controversial. Advocates of it insist that it helps older children accept a new sibling; opponents fear that children may be traumatized by seeing so much blood and pain.

If you are contemplating having an older child attend your birth you'll want to read *Birth—Through Children's Eyes*, edited by Sandra Van Dam Anderson, R.N., M.S., and Penny Simkin, P.T. This provides a thorough analysis of all the pros, cons, and special considerations of having a child attend delivery. If you then decide you want your child present, give him or her *Mom and Dad and I Are Having a Baby!* by Maryann Malecki, C.N.M., M.S.N., a book that, using a child's language, explains the whole birth process. The text is two-tiered in complexity so it's suitable for children as young as two or as old as ten. Either book can be ordered from Pennypress Inc., 1100 23rd Avenue East, Seattle, WA 98112, 206-325-1419.

ﻬ *Your Diet*

EATING TO PREVENT HEARTBURN

During the last months of pregnancy, many women find that heartburn, which is a raw, hot sensation felt in the chest usually after eating, becomes a frequent problem. There are two reasons why, at this time, you may be more prone to heartburn (which is not a heart disorder but a digestive problem).

As the growing baby begins to crowd the stomach entrance, it becomes harder for food to move its way downstream. That means food stays in your esophagus longer, causing irritation and a burning feeling. At the same time, hormones have relaxed the muscles that separate your esophagus from your stomach, so food and digestive juices can easily flow in reverse, going from your stomach back into the esophagus, causing painful inflammation.

To head off heartburn, you may not only need to change what you eat, but how you eat. Eating too quickly, for instance, can cause heartburn, as can gulping down drinks instead of sipping them. It helps to chew food thoroughly and to eat, if possible, in a calm setting. Eating small, lighter, frequent meals rather than large heavy ones once or twice a day is also an effective deterrent to indigestion.

A traditional heartburn preventive is to drink a cup of hot water with one tablespoon of lemon juice before every meal. The following foods also seem to trigger heartburn: spicy food, greasy foods, coffee, chocolate, carbonated drinks, cabbage, beans, and other gas-producing foods. If nighttime indigestion is a problem, sleeping propped up on pillows can help.

Overall, it's easier to avoid heartburn symptoms than it is to cure or relieve them once they've surfaced. There are some antacids that appear to be safe to use during pregnancy (ask your doctor), but you might want to try a folk remedy many people swear by first: peppermint tea. A cup of camomile tea is purported by some to give relief, too. And once you are suffering from heartburn, it's best to keep upright (not lie down) since, that way, gravity can help food make its passage downward.

ừ Your Workout

TONING THE PELVIC-FLOOR MUSCLES

The pelvic-floor (puboccoccygeus) muscles support your urethra, vagina, and rectum; they stretch from your pubic bone to your tailbone, forming a taut sling that serves as a "floor" to all your pelvic organs. During and after pregnancy, it's especially important to keep these muscles well conditioned, for several reasons.

As your uterus expands, it puts pressure on your bladder; as a result, many women find that they not only need to urinate more frequently in the last trimester, but they leak a little urine when they cough, sneeze, or laugh. Keeping the pelvic-floor muscles, which control the flow of urine (they are the muscles you relax in order to urinate, then contract to stop the flow), strong and toned can help prevent or minimize the problem of urinary incontinence.

In addition, during childbirth the pelvic-floor muscles often get strained from the pressure of the baby's head as it descends down the vaginal canal. But if these muscles are in good shape, they will be elastic enough to stretch and accommodate the baby's passage without tearing or being permanently displaced. When toned, the pelvic-floor muscles also easily contract back into position postpartum, thus ensuring that the vaginal canal resumes its original, snug shape. In contrast, when the pelvic-floor muscles are not kept in good condition, pre- and post-childbirth, the inner vagina may become widened, loose, and overstretched.

To keep the pelvic-floor muscles in shape you need to do Kegel exercises, exercises named after the California physician Arnold Kegel, who first identified the importance of the pelvic-floor muscles. Here is one version of a Kegel exercise (all versions are equally simple): progressively tighten the muscles surrounding your vagina and rectum to the count of ten; then release them to the count of five. You can do this anywhere, in any position, without anyone knowing that you're exercising. Each Kegel exercise should only take a few seconds; try to do at least ten over the course of a day.

Note: A common myth or misunderstanding is that "Kegeling" regularly will ensure that you won't need an episiotomy. An episiotomy is a surgical incision made during delivery (see pp. 183–85) to widen the vaginal opening or outlet; Kegel exercises promote flexibility and strength primarily in the inner vagina.

❧ Your Feelings

THE PREGNANT FATHER

When you consider the "couvade syndrome," there's no doubt that pregnancy can be a deeply emotional experience for men. Although study findings vary widely, the lowest estimates are that 20 percent of all fathers-to-be suffer from couvade—a syndrome in which a man actually experiences many of the physical complaints common to pregnancy. Many expectant dads, in other words, suffer from morning sickness, sleeping difficulties, food cravings, backaches, moodiness, chronic fatigue, and weight gain (ten pounds on average) during their wives' pregnancies. No underlying medical cause can be found for these symptoms, which invariably clear up after birth.

Couvade (from the French *couver*, meaning "to hatch"), has been noted in medical literature since the seventeenth century, and seems to represent a man's unconscious attempt to identify with his wife and to be involved in the pregnancy. Some researchers (and wives) also suspect couvade is a way of begging for attention—a psychological cry for some equal coddling.

Impending parenthood can change men in other ways, too. Many take pride in their new role as father-to-be and find that they feel much more protective of their wives (which can be a little irritating if you're accustomed to being independent and self-sufficient). Feeling jealous of the attention lavished on you and of the fact that your energies aren't completely centered on him is common; worries about money, the relentless responsibility, and the baby's health seem to be practically universal among fathers-to-be, too.

In fact, all the doubts and fears that have crossed your mind are likely to have crossed his. But where you may feel free to share and verbalize your emotions, many men feel that if they share their anxieties they'll seem uncommitted or weak. Some men also report that their wives won't listen to their fears. I know I was a bit guilty of that. While I welcomed my husband's positive, supportive reactions, I found his worries very threatening. In a sort of infantile way, I wanted him to simply reassure me, not to have any anxieties of his own. I found I really had to force myself to listen to him and not isolate him by refusing to deal with his concerns.

The pregnant partnership. Particularly as you near the end of pregnancy, you may find you and your partner have different psychological impulses and needs. You may feel a desire to "clear the deck" of commitments, tasks, and responsibilities as a way of getting ready for the baby's arrival. In contrast, you may find your partner suddenly stays late at the office, plunges into lots of new projects, and/or takes on lots of extra work. His impulse may be to avoid thinking about things he has no control over, such as medical complications. And, he may find concentrating on work is easier than dwelling on worries (about how he'll perform during labor and delivery, whether he'll love the baby, how good a father he'll be, and so on).

In the last weeks of my pregnancy, my husband seemed to want to seize the "good old days": he wanted to eat out, see movies, and visit friends a great deal. He felt, I think, like having a last "fling" as an unfettered couple. I, on the other hand, felt vulnerable and wanted quiet, privacy, and unscheduled evenings so I could collect myself for the upcoming labor and delivery.

Simply accepting that your partner's drives may be different from yours at this point in the pregnancy and that his different needs don't constitute a rejection or desertion of you can go a long way toward ensuring that you don't end up squabbling constantly. Also, it helps to be forewarned that, for many couples, the last months and especially weeks of pregnancy can be tense; not only do labor and delivery worries loom large, but your tendency to scrutinize each other in new ways may escalate (for example, you may never have minded his habit of being late before, but now find it irritating because you think of the "example" it will set for your baby-to-be). If you can remind yourself that both your husband's and your perspective may be a little bit skewed right now, you'll be better able to resist blowing differences out of proportion and take them in stride.

ೋ Your Life-Style

THINKING AHEAD ABOUT CIRCUMCISION

For many parents-to-be, there's really nothing to think about: they already know that if their baby is a boy, he will be circumcised. Many Jewish parents, for example, automatically choose circumcision for religious reasons; in most Moslem cultures, circumcision is an important tradition, too. But if you are not sure whether you would want a son to be circumcised, now is the time to give the issue careful thought. Making a choice for or against circumcision can be difficult, since so much of the evidence and expert advice is conflicting.

The foreskin has not been surgically removed from the penis of this newborn.

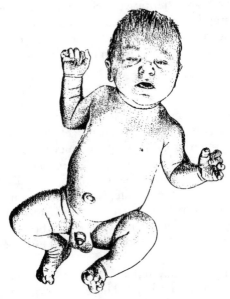

A circumcised newborn. The foreskin has been removed from his penis, which gives it an acorn-like appearance.

What is circumcision? It's an elective surgical procedure in which the foreskin (prepuce) of the penis is removed. The baby is strapped down on a special Y-shaped tray. Anesthesia is not usually given. After the genitals are swabbed with antiseptic, the foreskin is clamped to pull it away from the glans; then, a scalpel is inserted to cut the foreskin away. Bleeding is not usually profuse; ointment and gauze is used to wrap the penis after the procedure, which takes under fifteen minutes to perform.

For the past two decades the stance of the American Academy of Pediatrics (AAP) was that "there are no valid medical indications" for routine circumcision of the newborn. But in March 1989, due to new study findings, it altered its policy statement to say that circumcision "has potential medical benefits and advantages" as well as "inherent disadvantages and risks." In essence, the AAP chose not to choose: it straddles the fence and does not make a strong recommendation either for or against circumcision. That's primarily because so much of the evidence, pro and con, is, in the words of the AAP, "conflicting," "inconclusive," and "tentative." So, if you still feel indecisive after reviewing the catalog of pros and cons outlined ahead, give yourself some time and don't feel bad—even the nation's leading pediatric organization couldn't take a firm position on the issue.

The case for it

1. Circumcision makes it easier to keep the glans clean, partly because there is no foreskin to push back during washing. However, even staunch proponents of circumcision admit that proper penile hygiene can easily be taught to little boys.

2. Circumcision early in life eliminates the slight risk that it might be required later in life, when the trauma and risk of surgery and recovery are much greater. Circumcision is sometimes recommended for older boys or men who have phimosis—a rare problem in which the foreskin can't be retracted or drawn back.

3. Circumcision may reduce the risk of urinary tract infections (UTIs) in infant boys. These infections are of concern because not only do they invariably require antibiotic treatment, but, if they are not diagnosed early, the bacteria that causes them

could potentially spread and damage other organs, primarily the kidneys. Two studies conducted in U.S. Army hospitals indicated that in the first year of life, uncircumcised boys suffered from UTIs about eleven times more than circumcised ones. Yet because of methodological problems inherent in the study, these findings are still considered "tentative" by most independent experts.

4. Penile cancer, a type of cancer that occurs in old age and affects fewer than 1 male per 100,000, may occur at a higher rate in uncircumcised males. Yet, according to the American College of Obstetricians and Gynecologists (ACOG, whose members perform circumcisions), good hygiene can be just as good a cancer-preventive method. ACOG states that "although there may be a protective factor, the risks of complications from circumcision are greater than the risk of penile cancer in an uncircumcised male."

The case against it

1. It's painful—why else would babies scream in protest? Surprisingly, this has only recently been acknowledged. A new local anesthesia technique called a "dorsal penile nerve block" is being tested, but the AAP cautions that the block is "not without risk" and, until more studies are conducted, the AAP does not recommend its routine use.

2. Complications, although uncommon, are possible. Excessive bleeding (which may require stitches or even a blood transfusion) and infection (which usually requires antibiotic treatment) are the most common problem. Cases of penile "trauma"—incidences in which the penis is permanently damaged in some way—have been reported but are extremely rare.

3. It's an unnecessary medical expense. Blue Shield insurance plans in five states as well as Prudential Health Insurance no longer reimburse for this operation.

4. The foreskin is a normal piece of tissue that does not need to be removed. Plus, it serves to protect the meatus (the opening of the urethra) from diaper irritation, which can cause ulcerations and infection. At least one study supports the contention that the foreskin may be protective for at least the first year of life.

What to do. Since the medical facts are not persuasive enough to warrant a blanket recommendation either for or against circumcision, you may find you end up making your decision based on social or emotional considerations. Some men and women, for instance, want their sons to be circumcised to resemble their dads; others opt not to circumcise because they simply can't bear the thought of putting their infant "under the knife" with no anesthesia. It's a good idea to discuss the subject with your obstetrician (who, if you're not having a religious circumcision, is the person likely to perform the operation). In addition, if you want more information, the following pamphlets are free if you

---

₰   SERIOUS DOUBTS AND SILLY SUPERSTITIONS   ₰

Even as the "fetus" increasingly becomes "your baby" in your mind, you may be surprised to find that you still have occasional doubts about what you've gotten yourself into. Yet it's common to have misgivings about the wisdom of bringing a child into such a violent world; about the stability of your marriage and its ability to withstand the stresses of parenthood; about how good a parent you will be. In my last trimester, I sometimes felt trapped in an irrevocable decision: at times I found it chilling to think that the next twenty years of my life would not be my own.

In addition, many couples, despite themselves, find they buy into age-old superstitions. For example, some couples won't bring any baby items into their house before the birth for fear of bringing on bad luck; others won't choose their baby's name beforehand because of worry that doing so will "tempt fate."

Psychologists who have studied pregnancy consider these kinds of last-minute doubts and superstitions a "natural phenomenon"; they believe these feelings have an adaptive function in that they serve to increase your preparedness for the responsibilities and the emotional experience of parenthood. So, you shouldn't increase your worries by worrying about the fact that you're worrying. Having misgivings is normal and doesn't reflect at all on how you'll actually feel once your baby is born.

send a stamped, self-addressed envelope with your request: "Circumcision: A Personal Choice" (American College of Obstetricians and Gynecologists, Resource Center, 409 12th Street, S.W., Washington, DC 20024); "Care of the Uncircumcised Penis" (American Academy of Pediatrics, Dept. C, P.O. Box 927, Elk Grove Village, IL 60009).

9

MONTH EIGHT

(31½ to 36 WEEKS)

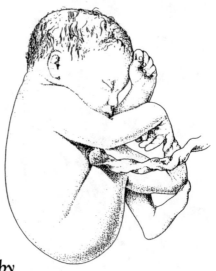

?• *Your Baby*

WEIGHT: 3½ to 6 pounds
LENGTH: 16 to 18 inches

In this as well as in the last month of pregnancy, the fetus stockpiles fat underneath its skin, rapidly gaining in both weight and height. It has very little in the way of developing left to do. The digestive tract and lungs are fully matured and all the bones are hardened, with the notable exception of the skull plates. The five bone plates that make up the skull stay flexible and unjoined so that they can safely slide together, even overlap, when pushed through the birth canal. The tighter the squeeze through the birth canal, the more molded or "pointy" the newborn's head will be. But the plates don't keep their elongated shape for long; within a few days after birth, the newborn's head becomes more rounded.

❧ *Your Body*

NINE EVENTS THAT SIGNAL LABOR IS NEAR

Most women get at least a few hints that labor is soon to start. My labor seemed to begin with a bang, but in retrospect all the clues that labor was about to begin were there. I simply hadn't paid attention to them (probably because I had convinced myself that I was going to deliver late, not, as it turned out, three weeks early).

The signs below are all "premonitory." Some of them will give you quite a good estimate of when you can expect labor to start, although none provide on-the-hour preciseness.

1. *Lightening.* Two to three weeks prior to labor, your baby may get into position for birth by dropping lower, headfirst, into your pelvis. You will probably feel that this has happened, since, as a result, you'll be able to breathe easier and, since pressure increases on the bladder, you'll have to urinate more often. In addition, when your doctor measures the height of your fundus (see "Your Doctor Appointment," p. 90), it will have decreased. But if you don't experience "lightening" it doesn't mean your labor is still weeks away. In many cases it only occurs after labor has begun.

2. *Braxton Hicks contractions.* These uncoordinated tightenings, which serve to tune up the uterus for the real thing, may increase in number and intensity the closer you get to labor. In fact, they can be easy to mistake for initial, early labor pains. But Braxton Hicks contractions are irregular in length, strength, and frequency; they stop if you change activity (if you lie down after walking, for instance, or vice versa) and although they can be painful, the pain is usually felt in the groin and lower abdomen. In contrast, real contractions are relatively regular (but far from clockwork-regular as most women will testify); no matter what you do, they won't stop; and the pain is usually experienced first in the back, radiating to the front. Over time, too, real contractions won't subside—they will get fiercer and more frequent.

3. *Increased backache.* A low, dull backache or crampiness akin to gas pains often signals that labor is just beginning or will begin within the day.

4. *Weight loss.* You may experience a one- to two-pound weight loss the week before delivery, since hormonal shifts sometimes trigger fluid loss.

5. *Increased vaginal discharge.* Several days prior to labor's commencement, you may notice an increasing amount of or one big blob of mucoid discharge that is clear, pink, or blood-tinged. This is the expulsion of the mucus plug, the thick barrier that protects and closes off the uterus throughout pregnancy. Many women only pass their mucus plug mid-labor. Also, any discharge that doesn't have a mucuslike quality but is bright red or heavy and menstrual-like should be reported immediately to your doctor.

6. *Cervical changes.* Your cervix may dilate slightly the week before delivery. Ask your doctor if he or she sees any signs of this when you get examined.

7. *Energy spurt.* Twenty-four to forty-eight hours beforehand you may feel charged with energy to clean and get things in order. However, not all women feel this "nesting" instinct.

8. *Gastrointestinal upset.* You may have frequent, loose bowel movements the day before labor begins (nature's way of ensuring your bowels are empty during labor). Also, you may experience diarrhea and vomiting at the beginning of and/or during labor.

9. *Rupture of membranes or "breaking the bag of waters."* In the majority of pregnancies, the sac of amniotic fluid the baby floats in doesn't rupture until late in labor. But in about 10 percent of pregnancies these membranes rupture prior to labor's onset. The waters may come in a warm, nonstop trickle or in a big gush. Either way, labor usually will begin within twenty-four to forty-eight hours.

Notify your doctor right away if you rupture your membranes. Also, note what the waters look like. They should be clear or yellowish, odorless or sweet-smelling. Waters that are dark brown, greenish, bloody or strong-smelling may signal fetal distress and so you should get to your doctor or to the hospital immediately.

The Two Sure Signs
That Labor Has Actually Begun

While lots of events may signal that labor is not far away, only two establish that it has truly, definitely begun.

Regular Contractions

What precisely is a contraction? It's a tensing-up of the uterine muscle. But unlike other muscles in your body, the uterine muscle fibers don't go back to their original size after flexing. Instead, they shorten in length, which means the upper portion of the uterus progressively decreases in size. This causes the baby to be pushed downward, toward the birth canal.

Contractions, then, supply the power that makes birth possible. The energy generated by contractions transforms your cervix into a birth canal (see pp. 150–51), forces your baby to enter your pelvis, propels him or her to actually be delivered, then stimulates the placenta to separate and be expelled.

Contractions have five features. They are:

1. Involuntary. You can't will them to start or stop. However, you can "encourage" them to quickly progress by walking around and remaining active for as long as possible during labor.

2. Intermittent. Contractions last between fifteen seconds (usually at the beginning of labor) and ninety seconds (toward the end). In between, your uterus is relaxed and you feel no pain at all. In the early stages of labor, these intervals may be between fifteen and thirty minutes long; toward the very end, they may only be two to three minutes apart.

3. Of increasing intensity. As labor progresses, contractions go from mild to moderate to strong. The stronger the contraction, the greater the progress of labor (it's much like driving a car: the more you step on the gas, the farther and faster you go). So although stronger contractions cause more intense pain, they are beneficial in that they bring you increasingly closer to the end of labor and the birth of your baby.

4. Of quite distinctive character. A contraction—and the pain it causes—is like a wave: it builds (as the uterine muscle begins to tense), crests (as it reaches complete flexure), and ebbs

ᘉ   *SPEEDING UP A SLOW LABOR*   ᘉ

Sometimes labor doesn't jog along at a steadily progressing pace. But when it does slow down, there are steps you can take that can often help to get it going again:

• Walk between contractions, then lean against a wall or hold on to a chair back, if necessary, during them. The force of gravity (which you take advantage of when you're upright) helps increase contraction strength.

• Urinate frequently, since a full bladder can slow down the action of your uterus. Similarly, a full bowel can slow things up. So if you haven't experienced diarrhea and/or haven't had a bowel movement during labor, you may want to think about having an enema.

• Stimulate your nipples by tugging and massaging them firmly but gently. This stimulates the production of the hormone oxytocin—the hormone responsible for triggering uterine contractions.

When these measures aren't effective, your doctor may suggest labor be sped up by artificially rupturing your membranes in a simple procedure called an amniotomy. To do this, a small plastic hook is inserted through your cervix, where it catches a small corner of your "bag of waters" and tugs it open. The procedure is painless, but it should be used as a last resort. If done too early in labor, it predisposes you to infection and also puts you on a path where more and more medical interventions may become necessary. For example, if the amniotomy doesn't speed things up (sometimes it doesn't), because of the infection risk you may need to speed things up with the drug Pitocin. Pitocin can make contractions unusually fierce, which can make it likely you'll need a painkiller. And whenever you take a painkiller during labor your risk of a cesarean delivery is slightly increased. Although this is a "worst-case" scenario, if your baby is not in distress it illustrates why it's best to try to speed labor along using nonmedical methods for as long as possible.

(as the muscle relaxes). So once you're at the acme or peak of a contraction, the pain begins to subside.

5. Regular. Contractions are usually described as being precisely rhythmic, separated by equally timed intervals. But I think it is better to think of "regular" in a more generalized way, since few women I know have had such clockwork-regular contractions. My late labor contractions, for example, came at varying intervals of two, three, and four minutes.

Cervical Effacement and Dilatation

Normally, the cervix (which is the neck of the uterus) is a thick, half-inch-long channel with a slight opening. But during labor, the power of contractions serves to soften, thin out, shorten (or "efface"), and widen ("dilate") your cervix. And by doing all this, a birth canal is created.

The process of effacement, in which the cervix shortens and becomes almost paper thin, is frequently halfway finished before labor even begins. Effacement is measured in percentages: when your cervix is fully effaced, it has thinned out 100 percent.

Dilatation, the process in which your cervix opens and widens, may start a little before labor, too. Dilatation is measured in centimeters (one centimeter equals approximately one-quarter inch). When you are four centimeters dilated, you are "officially" in labor; when you are ten centimeters dilated, your cervix is fully opened and your baby is ready to be pushed through the birth canal.

The Five Phases of Labor and Delivery

No description of labor and delivery can act as "fortune-teller" to reveal what childbirth will be like for you. But by familiarizing yourself with the medical details of childbirth and by learning what the range of possibilities are, you achieve something very important. You reduce the likelihood that you'll get stuck in a web of panicked questions ("What's happening?" "What does that mean?") during labor. The more you know, in other words, the less distracted you'll be by wild, unfounded fears and the more you'll be free to focus on yourself and the hard work at

THE BIRTH OF A BABY

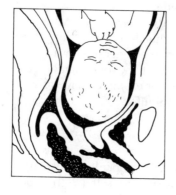

The cervix in late pregnancy before labor

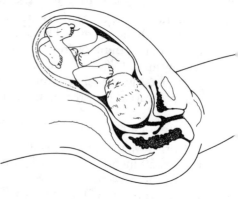

The cervix begins to efface (thin out) and dilate (open) in the first phase of labor.

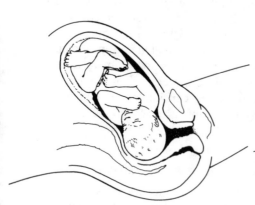

By the end of Phase Three of labor, the cervix is completely dilated and the baby begins to rotate to get ready to pass through the birth canal.

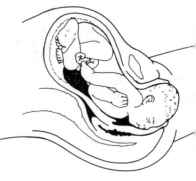

As the fourth, or "pushing," phase of labor draws to a finish, the baby's head crowns—i.e., it reaches the pelvic floor and can be seen at the vaginal opening.

hand. Simply, knowledge allows you to concentrate on your labor and delivery experience and helps prevent that experience from being taken over and dominated by doctors, nurses, machines, and uninformed worries.

Note: Conventionally, labor is described in three stages. The first stage comprises your entire labor; the second stage encompasses delivery; and in the third stage, the placenta is delivered. But I always find descriptions that rely on this division a little confusing, because they have to include too many subdivisions (they require explanations, such as, "Now, in the second phase of the first stage of labor . . ."). That's why, in my description, I've chosen not to use the major divisions of "stages." Instead, I've simply linked the subdivisions together to create *the five phases of labor*. Each phase corresponds to time-honored landmarks in the progress of a normal labor and delivery. Each phase has a medically clear-cut beginning and ending, too.

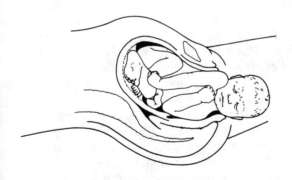

Once the baby's head is born, the shoulders and the rest of the body slide out quickly and easily.

Phase One: Early Labor

- **What happens:** Your cervix effaces (thins out) and dilates from zero to four centimeters. The contractions that bring about these changes usually last fifteen to twenty seconds, occur at fifteen- to thirty-minute intervals, and are quite mild—so mild, you may not even notice you're having them. In addition, your waters may break, your mucus plug may be loosed, and you may experience a little diarrhea.

- **How long it takes:** Early labor can last up to twenty hours or it can last a mere hour or two. In general, it's the longest part of labor, but luckily, it is also the easiest and least uncomfortable part (although the anticipation of more intense pain can make it a stressful time). In fact, you may only realize you are experiencing early labor as it nears its end.

- **Characteristic sensations:** You may feel a generalized discomfort in your pelvic region: mild menstrual-like or intestinal cramps and/or a nagging backache. Most women tolerate these symptoms quite well—they easily can continue with normal activities and don't need any breathing techniques to help them work through discomfort.

  When you finally realize "This is it!" you may feel excited, nervous, anxious. My first reaction was panic: I thought, "This can't be true, I'm not ready yet, I need more time!" (Of course, I eventually did face the fact that once labor has begun, there is no turning back, and was able to calm down.)

- **What you should do:** This is the time to pack your bags for the hospital, to make any last-minute preparations, to contact your labor coach, and to contact your baby-sitter (if you have children who are at home). Standard counsel is to rest or take a nap, but you may find you are too filled with anticipation for that. As an alternative, walking can be calming, can make you feel more comfortable, and will help your labor to progress (which means your labor will be shorter). If you feel panicked, try doing the "slow chest breathing" described on p. 177.

As far as eating and drinking are concerned, there are different views. Some physicians still recommend you have nothing to eat or drink at all as soon as you become aware that you are in labor. The basis for this advice is that it reduces the risk that you will inhale vomit (which can lead to pneumonia and even death) in the event that general anesthesia is necessary. But others point out that it is rare that general anesthesia is necessary during childbirth and that, even if general anesthesia is needed, precautionary measures need to be taken anyway since there is no guarantee a woman's stomach will be empty. In addition, critics of the "no food/no drink" advice point out that labor can be even harder if a woman must fight hunger pains, too.

Your digestion slows down and eventually shuts down completely during labor, so rich, heavy foods can make you feel nauseated and cause you to vomit. Light, simple broths, pastas or rice dishes, cottage cheese, yogurt, bread, and non-citrus fruits and juices are usually your best choices, but ask your doctor first.

Phase Two: Active Labor

● **What happens:** Your cervix dilates from four to eight centimeters. Contractions become more frequent, longer, and stronger; they usually come every two to five minutes and last forty-five to sixty seconds. In addition, you may experience nausea and vomiting as your digestion slows; your waters may break and/or your mucus plug may become loosed if they haven't already; and you may perspire heavily.

● **How long it takes:** Some labors are prolonged, some are very rapid, and others seem to stop and go. But on average the cervix dilates one centimeter per hour during active labor, which means this phase generally lasts three to five hours.

● **Characteristic sensations:** As active labor progresses, contractions get sharper, stronger, and more uncomfortable. Backache pain and feelings of pressure in your abdomen may increase. You may moan and your whole body may "tremble" or shake slightly as you reach the crest of a contraction.

At this time, you're unlikely to be talkative; instead, you'll be intense as you focus exclusively on yourself, on coping with what you're feeling and on your breathing techniques (at this point you may need to do "shallow chest breathing"—see p. 178—to get through contractions). You probably won't be in the mood for jokes; you're much more likely to be somewhat irritable and impatient, especially if you're kept waiting or you don't feel you're receiving enough help or attention. And especially, as you near the end of this phase, you may begin to feel unsure of yourself, to doubt your ability to keep coping.

• **What you should do:** Most doctors will tell you to notify them when your contractions are five minutes apart. Especially if you live more than a half hour away from the hospital, you may be advised to head for the hospital or birthing room immediately. However, if you live close by, many doctors and midwives advise you to stay at home for as long as you can take it, since you still may have a few hours of labor to go and you'll be much more comfortable and freer to move around at home.

If you're having your baby at a hospital, here are the steps you'll probably go through:

1) If you are preregistered (you usually do this one month in advance of your due date), you can go directly to the labor area. Otherwise, you or your partner may need to stop at the front desk to do admittance paperwork.

2) Once in the labor/delivery area, you usually will go to a special admitting room where you are asked questions about your health history and labor "symptoms."

3) You are assigned to a labor room where a nurse checks your blood pressure, pulse, temperature, and heartbeat. Then, either your doctor or a hospital physician will feel your abdomen to assess the position of the baby, and a vaginal exam is done, too, to see how dilated your cervix is.

4) A labor nurse—someone who not only keeps tabs on your vital signs but who provides support and encouragement as you work through contractions—is assigned to you. (In some cases, your doctor will act as your "labor nurse.")

5) Once your baby has fully descended down the birth canal, you usually are transferred to a delivery room, where your baby will be born.

If you are having your baby at a birthing center, you will usually be assigned upon entering to a midwife, who will do all medical checks and who will stay with you as you labor and deliver in the same room.

Phase Three: Hard Labor (or Transition)

- **What happens:** Your cervix dilates from eight centimeters to ten centimeters (ten centimeters is full dilation). Strong contractions may last as long as ninety seconds and may occur every one and a half to three minutes. They may come on so fast that there is no pause in between. In some cases, contractions will double-peak: they'll crest, subside momentarily, then crest again before fully subsiding. You may also experience some nausea and vomiting, leg and/or buttock cramps, hot and cold flashes, heavy perspiration, and/or shaking in your legs. Your water may break if it hasn't previously.
- **How long it takes:** Hard labor rarely lasts longer than an hour and a half, and it usually lasts under an hour. In many cases, hard labor is over within fifteen to twenty contractions.
- **Characteristic sensations:** Contraction pain and, for some women, back pain, is all encompassing—working through the pain will take your full effort and concentration. You may feel exhausted, short-tempered, panicked, and/or discouraged. In fact, just when you're ready to crumble—to insist that you can't take it anymore—the worst is probably over.
- **What you should do:** If you aren't there already, you should be on your way to the hospital or birthing center, since before long, you'll be ready to push your baby out. If you feel the urge to push before you have reached your birthing destination, "blow through" your contractions. It is impossible to push and bear down when you are blowing through your mouth in fast puffs.

Phase Four: Birth

- **What happens:** The baby descends down the birth canal (which is about four inches long). At the end of this phase, your baby is born.

Contractions slow, spacing out to two to five minutes apart, lasting sixty to ninety seconds. During each contraction, the baby moves down the birth canal a little further, although at the end of each contraction the baby also backslides a little. The progress of the baby through the birth canal is described in terms of stations, from zero to four. At four, the baby's head bulges at the vaginal opening and doesn't recede: this is called crowning and is a signal that your baby will slide out completely within a minute or two. At this point, if your vaginal opening isn't large enough to accommodate the baby's head without tearing, an episiotomy (see pp. 183–85) may be performed.

During this phase you probably will feel an overpowering desire to push—it's a feeling similar, but much stronger, to pushing out a bowel movement. When you bear down during contractions, it helps tremendously to speed up the birth, since the force of consciously contracted abdominal muscles increases the power generated by contractions.

- **How long it takes:** The baby may descend quickly and be born in just a push or two, or the descent may take up to two hours. Although many doctors feel that pushing efforts shouldn't last more than two hours, there is no evidence that there is any harm in them taking longer, as long as there is progress and no signs of fetal distress.

- **Characteristic sensations:** The overwhelming urge to push may provide a distraction from contraction pains (which tend to be less intense now). As the baby moves down the birth canal, you may feel some burning and stretching, but these sensations tend to be fleeting since the pressure of the baby's head on tissues has a natural numbing effect.

At first, your pushing efforts may be clumsy and uncoordinated (I had to ask a nurse, "How do I push, I can't remember"). Although some women never feel the urge to push, others find the feeling is frightening because it is so powerful and all-encompassing.

If this phase is prolonged, you may feel discouraged, not to mention exhausted. Some women are able to doze in between contractions, though, and many do find they eventually get a second wind.

- **What you should do:** If the baby's descent is taking a long time, change positions frequently (most women bear down most effectively when in a squatting position). Most delivery rooms are equipped with mirrors so that you can actually see your baby being delivered. Don't be squeamish about looking. Also, if you wear eyeglasses, make sure your coach has prior instructions to bring them into the delivery room (my eyeglasses got left in the labor room and since I'm blind as a bat, my baby's birth was a blur). If you normally wear contact lenses, you'll need to bring eyeglasses, since most hospitals require contacts to be removed (just in case emergency anesthesia is needed) during labor and delivery.

Phase Five: Delivery of the Placenta

• **What happens:** Mild contractions resume after birth; these work to detach the placenta from the uterine wall and to expel it. Episiotomy incisions or tears are stitched after the placenta has been expelled.

Your uterus may be palpated and massaged externally, through your abdominal wall, by your doctor or midwife to encourage it to contract and to reduce the bleeding. In some cases, your doctor or midwife may need to insert his or her hand inside your uterus to ensure there is no tissue retained—this hurts, but only takes a few seconds.

• **How long it takes:** The placenta is usually expelled in five to sixty minutes.

• **What you should do:** Afterbirth contractions are mild compared to labor contractions. You may need to push once or twice to help deliver the placenta.

Ask your partner, doctor, or nurse for help in positioning your baby at your breast for nursing. Since you may have the chills (your whole body may shake and your teeth may chatter for a while after birth), you may want to ask for a blanket. You probably will feel hungry, thirsty, not to mention exhausted, sweaty, and sticky. Most nurses will give you a sponge bath in the recovery room, but you'll probably have to wait several hours before being allowed to shower. If you've delivered in a birthing center, though, you may be able to shower as soon as you feel like getting up.

COPING WITH "BACK" LABOR

How the fetus is positioned in your womb has a great impact on how easy or difficult your labor and delivery is. The position that is most common and easiest on you: the baby's head is down, the chin tucked in, the face directed toward your back. The position that makes labor harder and longer for you (it poses no threat to baby): the baby's head is down, its chin tucked in, but its face is directed toward your naval. That means the hard back of the baby's head presses into your lower spine with each contraction. As a result, you not only have contraction pain to contend with but strong back pain, too.

There are techniques, however, that can help you cope with this type of "back" labor. First and foremost: *don't lie on your back*. This increases the pressure on your spine, increases your pain, and prolongs your labor. Instead, kneel, squat, get on all fours, or lie on your side to get your weight off your spine. In addition, these tactics are usually helpful:

• Change positions and move around as much as possible. This will speed up your labor and ensure you don't get stuck in a position that is less than optimally comfortable.

• Try applying heat (in the form of hot towels, a heating pad, or hot-water bottle) to the small of your back (which is usually the locus of pain). If this doesn't help, sometimes cold (in the form of a cold-water bottle or ice cubes encased in plastic, then a towel) provides relief.

• Have your labor coach massage the area of your back where you feel the most pain. Simply applying strong steady pressure to the painful area, using the heel of the hands, is the most effective.

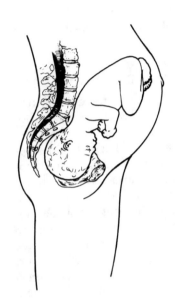 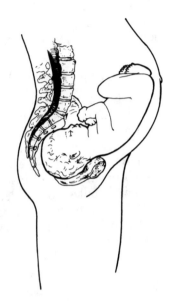

During "back" labor (left), the hard back of the baby's head presses into your lower spine, causing strong back pain. When the baby's face is directed toward your back (right), labor tends to be easier, with less intense lower-back discomfort.

❧ *Your Doctor Appointment*

ESSENTIAL ISSUES TO DISCUSS: CHILDBIRTH PAIN-RELIEF OPTIONS, COMMON HOSPITAL PROCEDURES

Now's the time to learn all you can (then to ask your caregiver any questions you may have) about pain and medication during childbirth and about common medical procedures done in the hospital. For example, you'll want to find out if your doctor prefers certain medications and in what circumstances he or she recommends using them. You'll also want to know what to expect when you admit yourself to the hospital: Is it standard to be given an enema? To have an IV drip? To use electronic fetal monitoring? And what choices do you have about these procedures? In addition, you'll want to let your caregiver know what is most important to you about the care you receive during labor and delivery.

Pain Relief During Labor and Birth

There is a good reason why natural, unmedicated childbirth is still the ideal: it is, without question, the least risky method of delivery for both mother and baby. The fact is, even the safest pain relievers have potential complications. That's why anesthesia is not "routine"—i.e., it's not automatically prescribed for every woman in labor. Instead, opting for anesthesia is a choice you make (unless, of course, it's a surgical birth).

Although you probably have some gut feelings about the subject of pain relief (you may desperately not want to resort to painkillers or you may be very drawn to the idea of a pain-free birth), it's best to keep as open a mind as possible before labor. That way, if your labor isn't "that bad" you won't prematurely request drugs nor, despite your wishes for a completely natural childbirth, feel deeply disappointed if it turns out you need help in the form of medication.

The Two Most-Used Pain Blocks

Demerol. This reduces the amount of pain you feel without making you feel too drowsy or "drugged." It doesn't offer total pain relief, but that is considered a positive attribute, since it means you are still able to participate effectively in the birth. When injected into an IV drip, Demerol takes effect within five minutes; effects last between two and four hours.

Demerol can cause maternal low blood pressure, but this can usually be quickly corrected by increasing intravenous fluids. Other side effects include nausea, vomiting, facial flushing, and dryness of the mouth.

The biggest risks of taking Demerol occur to the fetus, because the drug easily crosses the placenta and enters the fetus's bloodstream. Especially if administered one hour prior to delivery,

Demerol can depress the fetus's ability to breathe on its own (in which case a baby may need the help of an artificial respirator as well as drugs to counteract the effects of Demerol). To avoid this risk, most physicians try to administer Demerol well before (two to three hours) expected delivery (the problem with this—from the mother's point of view—is that the drug may wear off before she's been through the worst part of labor).

Even when Demerol is given several hours before delivery, though, it may have some effects on the fetus. Some babies exposed to Demerol are "floppy" limbed at birth; some are drowsy and unresponsive a day or two afterward.

Epidural anesthesia. The epidural block numbs you from the waist down yet leaves you fully awake. Because it is administered in frequent, small doses, the flow can be stopped just prior to delivery, allowing you to help push your baby out.

An epidural is usually only administered during Phase Two, Active Labor (not earlier, because it may inhibit labor progress, and not later, because it can impede your pushing efforts). Here's how it's administered: You lie on your left side or you sit up with your back arched as much as possible. Your lower back is

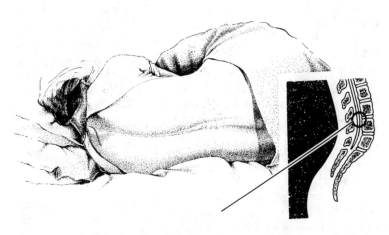

For an epidural to be set up, you usually need to lie on your side with your back arched as much as possible. The epidural space of your spine is circled on the inset; the bar points to the place between the vertebrae of your lower back where the epidural catheter is inserted.

cleansed, then a local anesthetic is injected to numb a small area (roughly one-half square inch). A large epidural needle is then introduced into the space around your spinal column; a long tube or catheter is threaded into the needle. This catheter stays in place until after birth (it's taped to your back—you don't feel it there and it doesn't prevent you from moving in your bed). Medication is injected into it.

The effect of an epidural is usually felt within a few minutes. Whenever it begins to wear off, a new dose is injected into the catheter. Besides numbing the nerves supplying the uterus (thus killing contraction pain), it also tends to cause loss of sensation in your legs.

The advantages of an epidural are that very little medication reaches the baby; the medication does not make you feel drowsy before or after the birth; and the medication dose can be lightened so that you are able to effectively bear down and push your baby out naturally. In fact, the epidural is the safest, most effective labor anesthesia available today.

An epidural, however, is not without some risk. The biggest is that it can "snowball" and lead to the use of more and more medical procedures. With an epidural, you can't walk to the bathroom or even feel the urge to urinate, so if your labor lasts more than a few hours, you may need to have your bladder emptied by means of urinary catheterization—a procedure that increases the risk of a postpartum urinary tract infection. If an epidural hampers your ability to really push, as it sometimes does, your baby is more likely to be delivered by forceps. Forceps delivery carries some risk to the baby (see pp. 185–86) and also requires you to have a large episiotomy. And when you have an epidural you must stay in bed for your entire labor and must have continuous electronic fetal monitoring, two factors which seem to increase your chances of having a cesarean section. In addition, many women find the epidural causes nausea and vomiting.

Several other problems have been associated with an epidural, although these are rare: a) there is the risk that the medication will be inadvertently injected into the spinal column, which can cause temporary total body paralysis and require emergency respiratory resuscitation; b) an epidural may cause a sudden drop in blood pressure, although this can usually be corrected before any harm is done to the fetus; and c) it may not work, or may only afford partial or patchy relief of pain.

Other Labor Medications

Sedatives and tranquilizers. These are usually prescribed in very early labor. They don't kill pain but relieve tension and promote sleep. On the positive side, these drugs can help you rest so that you're able to work with contractions when they get harder. This particularly makes sense if you're very apprehensive, nervous, and/or are experiencing a slow, prolonged early labor. Negatively, these drugs can cause nausea, vomiting, low blood pressure, and delirium. They cross the placenta and may cause temporary respiratory problems in the newborn as well as drowsiness in the first two days of life.

Pudendal nerve block. This is an injection into the inside wall of the vagina. It is usually done within an hour of delivery. It relaxes the perineum to make delivery faster and easier, plus reduces the pain of an episiotomy. It does not block contraction pain. Occasionally it fails to work; there is no risk to you or to the fetus.

Spinal or saddle block. This is an injection of local anesthesia into the spinal canal. It's done before delivery and numbs the lower part of the body (you can't feel your legs). The main advantage: it appears to have no effect on the fetus. The biggest drawback: it may cause severe postpartum headache.

General anesthesia. Today this is rarely used, except in emergency or complicated cesarean deliveries. You are completely unconscious. As long as the fetus is delivered quickly—within five minutes—the anesthesia should not have an effect on the newborn's health or behavior.

Common Hospital Procedures

Hospital rules and regulations are becoming increasingly more flexible, which means fewer procedures are mandatory for every laboring woman who walks in the door. Still, you will want to have your doctor note any special requests you may have on your medical chart (a copy of which is usually forwarded to the hospital's labor and delivery room one month prior to your due date). In many cases, your doctor will arrive considerably after your arrival, and it can be hard to fend off nurses and doctors who want to perform a procedure you want to avoid unless there's a written note on your medical record.

The procedures outlined below are commonly "routine" in hospitals; here's what they are and the arguments for and against them.

IV drip. To start an IV (intravenous) drip, a needle is inserted into a vein in the back of your hand or on the inside of your forearm; a thin, long tube is connected to the needle; then a bag of fluids (usually a solution of sugar water) is connected to the tube. If an emergency arises and you need medication or even a blood transfusion, this can be administered quickly through the IV. This is the chief reason doctors prefer you to have an IV in place; in addition, the fluids are believed to help prevent dehydration and to keep energy levels up, especially during long labors.

The alternate view is that a woman who is experiencing a normal, natural (i.e., unmedicated) labor can drink enough fluid to prevent dehydration and is unlikely to need emergency medication. The IV drip not only interferes with freedom of movement (although you can walk around, you must drag the stand that holds the fluids along with you), it impedes relaxation, too (since you may worry about tugging or pulling the IV line out).

The majority of doctors and hospitals feel quite strongly about the necessity for an IV drip during labor and will not allow you to forego one completely. If you find this is the case you may try to strike a bargain and see if you can at least wait to have one inserted until the very tail end of your labor.

Pubic-hair shave. Luckily, the mandatory shaving of a laboring woman's pubic hair on admittance is being phased out in most hospitals. It was common and standard because it was believed that a shave reduced the risk of infection if an episiotomy turned out to be necessary. But actually, it seemed to do more harm than good, with razor nicks and irritated hair follicles being more likely to lead to infection.

Vehemently protest if you discover shaving of pubic hair is still required at the hospital you plan to deliver in: not only is it unnecessary and embarrassing, it causes truly maddening postpartum itching.

Enema. Today, most doctors and hospitals don't routinely require enemas (they used to be routine because it was thought that if feces were expelled at the time of the baby's birth, the episiotomy site would be infected). But this doesn't mean an enema has no place whatsoever in labor care. For instance, if a woman has not had a bowel movement in twenty-four hours and is experiencing a long, slow labor, an enema can help speed things up. Also, the baby seems to pass through the birth canal easier if the colon is empty.

In addition, some women worry about the possibility of having a bowel movement during labor. They prefer having an enema and the assurance that their bowel is clear (although, nature often takes care of this problem by triggering diarrhea in the early phase of labor). But, the fact is that most women pass at least some fecal matter (even if they've had an enema or diarrhea) during the pushing stage; yet few women even realize this because they don't really feel the bowel movement and nurses are trained to instantly, automatically "whisk" the fecal matter away.

Electronic fetal monitoring. (EFM) The purpose of EFM is to check on the health of the fetal heart rate and to see how well the fetal heart responds to the stress of contraction pressure.

There are two types of EFM. One is external: Two belts, which are connected by tubes to a computerlike machine, are worn around your waist. One belt has an ultrasound device on it that picks up sound waves and thus records the fetal heartbeat. The other has a pressure-sensing device that records the length and strength of contractions.

The other type of EFM is internal. Internal monitoring tends to provide more accurate information. It also involves two monitoring devices. One is an electrode that is attached to the head of the fetus and records heart rate; the other is a catheter that is placed in the amniotic fluid and records contraction pressure. Both of these devices are threaded through your vagina (then taped to the inside of your thigh to hold them in place) and are connected to a computerlike monitoring machine. Because the technique is "invasive," internal monitoring is associated with a slightly increased risk of both fetal and maternal infection and there seems to be a slight risk of tissue injury to the fetal scalp and to the mother's uterus as well.

When a pregnancy is high risk (when labor is preterm or the mother has diabetes or heart disease, for instance) or if painkilling medication is being used, EFM is done almost continuously during labor. And in these situations the benefits of EFM are well documented. However, the use of EFM in a normally progressing, low-risk pregnancy is controversial.

Many health professionals use continuous EFM in all pregnancies because it makes them feel secure to know what the status of the fetal heart rate is at any given moment. Some women, too, find that monitoring provides reassuring information, and they appreciate the fact that the monitor lets them know ahead of time when a contraction is coming on.

But the benefits of EFM in low-risk pregnancy have not been established. In fact, several studies have not only found that there are *no* benefits but that EFM leads to unnecessary cesarean sections. This is probably because monitors seem to be less accurate when there's low risk and so they often indicate a problem when none exists.

Lawsuit jitters drive many hospitals to make EFM mandatory. If this is the case and/or if your doctor feels strongly about using EFM (and you are at low risk), you might try negotiating for noncontinuous, intermittent external EFM. If you're only hooked up to the monitor every half hour, for instance, instead of nonstop, you'll be much freer to move around during labor, and the machine and its beeping won't dominate your labor experience.

❧ Your Diet
(or, more accurately, Your Baby's Diet)

THINKING AHEAD ABOUT BREAST-FEEDING VERSUS BOTTLE-FEEDING

How you choose to feed your baby can be a surprisingly emotion-charged decision. Not only are others liable to have strong opinions about whether you should breast- or bottle-feed, you may experience a variety of conflicting feelings as you face the choice. Given this, it's important to keep these things in mind:

1. The health benefits to both mother and child of breast-feeding are so overwhelming that it makes sense to at least give it an honest trial. Also, you won't really know your true feelings about nursing until you've tried it. Before I had my baby, for instance, the whole breast-feeding thing seemed, at bottom, rather creepy. I was afraid it would hurt and I simply couldn't picture having a little creature tugging at my nipples. Postpartum, though, I experienced a complete turnaround and I found breast-feeding to be one of the most satisfying (not to mention inexpensive, convenient, easy, and painless) aspects of mothering in the early months.

2. Ultimately, though, you need to make the feeding choice that leaves you feeling comfortable and happy. Despite all the arguments in favor of breast-feeding, it really makes no sense at all if it leads you to feel uptight and resentful of the baby.

3. No matter what method of feeding you finally choose, you're likely to encounter criticism. For instance, women who breast-feed must deal with comments that aim to undermine their confidence, like, "Are you sure you're making enough milk?" Women who bottle-feed are frequently made to feel "second-rate" because they're giving their babies "second-best" milk. Why the world at large is so opinionated about how *you* feed *your* baby is hard to figure out, but being forewarned of this fact may help you deflect some of these barbs.

Here, then, is a thorough rundown of all the pros and cons of both breast- and bottle-feeding.

BREAST-FEEDING

Health Benefits to Baby

Not only does human milk contain components not found in the milk of other animals, it actually changes in composition as an infant matures, offering a baby the precise nutrition he or she needs at any given stage of development.

Breast milk supplies immunological factors that protect a baby from colds, allergies, diarrhea, and other ailments in the first three months. It is also easy to digest; nursed babies rarely suffer from constipation.

Studies suggest that children who are breast-fed for more than six months have about half the chance of developing childhood cancers of the lymph system as children who are bottle-fed or breast-fed for less time.

Prolonged nursing encourages good jaw and tooth formation; in a study of over nine thousand children, those who were bottle-fed were 40 percent

BOTTLE-FEEDING

Health Benefits to Baby

Although it's commonly been stated that bottle-fed babies tend to be fatter than breast-fed ones, the newest studies suggest that this isn't true.

Today's formulas imitate breast milk quite well and provide adequate, well-balanced nutrition.

If a mother is addicted to drugs or has had unusual exposure to an environmental contaminant, prepared formula would be the safer, healthier choice, since the level of toxins in her milk could be hazardous to the baby.

BREAST-FEEDING

Health Benefits to Baby

more likely to have misaligned teeth than children who nursed for at least a year.

Health Drawbacks for Baby

Since breast milk contains very little vitamin D, if a baby is rarely exposed to sunlight (a source of vitamin D), there is a chance that he or she could develop rickets—the vitamin D deficiency disease that impedes proper bone development. If a breast-fed baby doesn't get approximately one-half hour of sunlight exposure per week, a vitamin D supplement may be necessary to prevent the problem of rickets from occurring.

In extremely rare instances, a mother's milk lacks the mineral zinc—which can cause her baby to develop a skin rash and lead to loss of appetite, irritability, and stunted growth if not properly diagnosed. A zinc supplement quickly cures the problem.

BOTTLE-FEEDING

Health Drawbacks for Baby

Formula has no disease-protection properties (in general, studies show that bottle-fed babies are more likely to visit a doctor or stay in the hospital than breast-fed ones). Formula does not change in composition according to a baby's needs. There is a chance that as researchers discover new substances in breast milk, formula will turn out to be missing some elements of value. For all these reasons, the American Academy of Pediatrics urges that all infants, if possible, should be breast-fed for the first year.

Some babies are allergic to formula based on cow's milk. The symptoms are excessive crying, gas, stomach pain, and diarrhea. In most cases, treatment consists of changing to a soy-based formula.

BREAST-FEEDING

Again, in extremely rare instances, a mother's milk may cause breast-milk jaundice—a condition that is rarely serious and is simply treated by interrupting breast-feeding for two days (then resuming it).

Health Benefits for Mother

Nursing, which burns up approximately five hundred calories a day, helps metabolize the fat deposits that were acquired during pregnancy. In fact, many breast-feeding mothers find they shed their postpartum pounds within three to six months without much conscious effort.

Breast-feeding is what a woman's body is primed to do after delivery, so a nursing mother is unlikely to experience the painful engorgement that is common when breast-feeding is not chosen.

BOTTLE-FEEDING

Bottle-fed babies are less likely to have straight teeth; and if a baby is allowed to go to bed at night with a bottle in his or her mouth, the liquid in the bottle can bathe and seriously decay the baby's teeth.

Health Benefits for Mother

A woman does not need to delay diagnostic or treatment procedures that can't be safely begun while nursing. (For instance, some diagnostic tests involve the ingestion of radioactive drugs, which pass directly into a woman's milk and are potentially harmful to a baby.)

BREAST-FEEDING

Health Drawbacks for Mother

Women who breast-feed exclusively for over three months seem to experience bone loss in the lower spine, despite adequate calcium intake. However, this bone loss does not appear to be permanent; once nursing ends, it can be regained if a woman gets sufficient calcium and exercises moderately.

Although it is rare, some women contract infectious mastitis, a painful breast infection that is often accompanied by alternating fever and chills, fatigue and nausea. Antibiotic treatment is usually necessary. (In most cases it is not necessary to discontinue breast-feeding entirely.)

BOTTLE-FEEDING

Health Drawbacks for Mother

When a mother doesn't nurse, she may need to work more to regain her prepregnancy figure since postpartum pounds are less apt to simply melt away as they do when breast-feeding.

Many who do not breast-feed experience painful breast engorgement postpartum. Several major health organizations (including an FDA advisory panel) oppose the use of drugs to end lactation, since these drugs are thought to be minimally effective and yet are associated with a wide range of potentially serious side effects. In most cases, breast discomfort is best managed by applying ice packs to the breast, binding the breasts tightly, and/or taking mild painkillers.

BREAST-FEEDING

Practical Advantages

Breast milk cannot sour, be improperly mixed, overheated, or contaminated by poor sanitary conditions; it's always in a clean container and is always just the right temperature.

Breast-feeding is free and ecological; there are no bottles, formula, or nipples to buy and, eventually, discard.

It's quick, easy, and handy: no bottles to prepare, no formula to shop for, no feeding equipment to pack every time mother and baby go out. And, a mother can respond quickly to her baby's hunger cries, without having to stop and prepare a bottle.

Night feedings need hardly break a mother's slumber: she can just pick the baby up and put him or her to the breast. No trips to the refrigerator, no mixing, no warming, etc.

BOTTLE-FEEDING

Practical Advantages

As a general rule, bottle-fed babies need to eat less frequently than breast-fed ones, since formula takes longer to digest.

A mother who bottle-feeds is not tied down; other caregivers can as easily feed the baby as she can.

Bottle-feeding does not require a woman to buy any special blouses or bras.

A woman never has to worry about being discreet when bottle-feeding in public.

A woman can diet, drink, eat, and take medication without it having any direct ill effects on her baby's health.

Night feedings can be given by someone other than the mother, thus allowing her the freedom to sleep uninterrupted.

BREAST-FEEDING	BOTTLE-FEEDING

Practical Disadvantages

Breast-feeding must be learned: teaching a baby to "latch on" to the breast correctly takes practice; finding comfortable nursing positions takes some trial and error, and gaining confidence takes time.

A nursing mother is more tied down than one who bottle-feeds, especially in the first weeks when a newborn may need to nurse frequently, even every hour. However, it is possible for breast-feeding to be supplemented by bottle-feeding, thus freeing the mother up somewhat. Also, many women don't find being "tied down" is, overall, a disadvantage. Instead, they find nursing makes them feel needed—of unique importance—as well as deeply secure in their role of mother.

There may arise situations in which a mother may feel awkward about nursing in public.

For mothers who choose to supplement with bottles of expressed milk, it takes time to learn how to express milk and it then takes time to learn how to do it on a regular basis. Breast pumps range in

Practical Disadvantages

Formula is more expensive than breast milk and an ample supply must always be kept on hand.

Several sets of glass or plastic bottles (or bottles that use plastic liners) must be purchased; rubber nipples must be replaced every couple of months.

Bottles, formula, etc., must be prepared and packed whenever the baby is taken out.

BREAST-FEEDING	BOTTLE-FEEDING

Practical Disadvantages

price from inexpensive (under
$10 for a manual pump) to
quite pricey (over $150 for
some electric models).

Continuing to nurse and
going back to work can take
some juggling; expressing milk
during office hours can also be
logistically tricky. However,
many women find part-time
nursing is quite successful—
i.e., they nurse their babies in
the morning and night while
bottles of formula substitute
during the day.

A breast-feeding mother needs
to invest in nursing bras and
pads and shirts that button
down the front.

A breast-feeding mother needs
to watch her diet more carefully than one who doesn't
nurse: nursing mothers especially need to eat more
calcium-rich foods and to
drink plenty of liquids. Also,
a breast-feeding mother may
need to abstain from eating
certain foods that upset her
baby's digestion and/or affect
her baby's liking of her milk.
Finally, while breast-feeding, a
woman should not drink,
smoke, or take drugs.

BREAST-FEEDING	BOTTLE-FEEDING

Emotional Considerations

Women who breast-feed successfully usually describe it as a wonderful, satisfying experience. They are deeply moved by the warmth and closeness they establish with their infants and also feel a sense of contentment and pride in having been able to nurture and nourish their babies so well. Many mothers, in fact, look back at their nursing years with great joy and nostalgia.

On the other hand, nursing, when it doesn't go smoothly, can be a source of frustration and disappointment; it can make a woman feel inadequate, like a failure. For nursing to be successful and enjoyable, a woman must receive accurate information as well as encouragement. Plus, she must be willing to give it more than a perfunctory try, since without patience and commitment breast-feeding is likely to fail.

Emotional Considerations

With bottle-feeding, how much a baby drinks can be exactly measured, which may be reassuring to some mothers.

Some women feel a very deep aversion to breast-feeding, so much so that they are strongly reluctant to even give it a try. Obstetricians, pediatricians, and psychologists all agree that women who feel this way should choose bottle-feeding and should be supported in their choice, since it's best for the baby to have a mother who is happy and relaxed rather than one who is pressured, dissatisfied, and angry during feedings.

❧ *Your Workout*

RELAXATION AND BREATHING EXERCISES

In your childbirth education class, you'll be given instructions in both relaxation and breathing techniques. Most childbirth education instructors urge you to practice these techniques to an unrealistic degree (to a degree, in other words, that most couples simply don't have time for). The truth is that as long as you are somewhat familiar with the basic techniques—and have instructions at hand for when you actually go into labor—you'll be more than adequately prepared.

What follows is a description of the types of relaxation and breathing exercises used during labor. The patterns you learn in class may differ slightly, but you might want to run through these once so you have some alternative techniques to turn to, if needed, during labor.

Relaxation Sequence

Relaxation exercises aim to teach you what tense, taut muscles feel like and how to relax them. The underlying philosophy is that the more relaxed your whole body is during labor, the more likely it is that your uterus will contract unimpeded (and, thus, the less prolonged, tiring, and painful labor will be for you).

Put on loose, comfortable clothing. Recline in a cozy chair or prop yourself up with pillows on your bed. Relax as much as possible, making sure your breathing is slow, easy, and deep. Now, you're going to tighten, then release one muscle at a time, so that at the end of the sequence your whole body feels loose, like a rag doll. Starting from the soles.

As tightly as possible:

1. Scrunch your toes. Hold for a few seconds. Take a deep breath and exhale as you release (wiggle, roll, rotate, or gently shake the body part loose if it helps). Move on to next number, making sure as you progress, not to tense muscles you've already worked on.
2. Tense your feet.
3. Flex your calves.

4. Harden your thighs.
5. Pull in your buttocks.
6. Contract your vagina and rectum.
7. Suck in your stomach.
8. Tense your spine.
9. Clench your fists.
10. Stiffen your forearms.
11. Firm your upper arms.
12. Tense your arm sockets.
13. Hunch your shoulders.
14. Tense your neck.
15. Clench your jaw.
16. Scrunch your forehead.

Your whole body should feel deliciously limp, heavy, and loose now. This knowledge of how to relax your body will be especially useful in counteracting the tension that builds up in response to contraction pain.

Breathing Tactics

Breathing routines aim to help you maintain psychological control as well as to help you avoid hyperventilation (panicked breathing), which can make you feel faint. The routines described below are usually used during contractions; each tactic should be preceded (i.e., when you feel a contraction coming on) and followed (when the contraction ebbs) by a full, deep abdominal breath (breathe in deeply through your nose, so you feel your abdomen rise, then breathe out through your mouth so you feel your abdomen fall).

Slow Chest Breathing

Slowly and deeply inhale through your nose, counting forward to five; then, counting backward to zero, exhale through your mouth. Per minute you should be taking about eight to ten of these breaths. This type of breathing can help you keep your composure (when you may feel excited and/or panicked by the realization that you've actually begun labor), and it can be useful between contractions during advanced labor to help you keep your body relaxed.

Shallow Chest Breathing

Take short breaths through your mouth, which should be slack and relaxed, then push the breaths out through your mouth. If it helps, give the exhale a slight emphasis. The breaths should be rapid but rhythmic and evenly spaced (about one breath per two or three seconds). This technique becomes useful during the hard contractions of late-stage labor.

Pant-Blow Breathing

This is really a series of short pants punctuated by blows outward. The tactic is designed to help you resist the urge to bear down or push prematurely (since when you blow out, it is physically impossible to bear down or push). If the pushing urge is mild, follow this pattern: take three shallow breaths, inhale, then blow out, repeat. As the urge to push becomes more intense you may find you have to blow out with every breath to resist bearing down. (I'm positive that the only reason I didn't end up delivering my daughter during the cab ride to the hospital was because I knew how to "blow.")

➥ *Your Feelings*

WEIRD DREAMS AND FAILING MEMORY

Especially in the last months of pregnancy, many women have an abundance of mysterious, strange, and sometimes troubling dreams; they also find they're unusually forgetful during the day. The explanation for these occurrences is partly physical: sleep tends to be frequently disturbed (by a need to urinate, difficulty in finding a comfortable sleeping position, kicks from the baby, etc.) during late pregnancy, so you are 1) more likely to remember your dreams, since dream recall is its most vivid prior to wakings; and 2) you are more likely to suffer from fatigue and its side effect of forgetfulness during the day. But bizarre dreams and mild maternal "amnesia" are also barometers of your psychological state.

Various researchers have noted that pregnant women commonly have unsettling dreams involving voyages (in cars, boats, airplanes, and quite frequently through dark, endless tunnels), a theme that seems to be associated with an apprehension of impending labor and delivery. Anxiety dreams in which you forget your baby somewhere or are unable to save your baby from some danger seem to be quite common during pregnancy, too. These dreams probably reflect doubts and concerns you may have about your ability to be a good mother. Studies of the dreams of pregnant women have also found that images of dangerous, turbulent waters—emblematic perhaps of worries about the "breaking of waters" that occurs during labor—as well as images of domestic and wild animals—thought to be fetal symbols—are also universal.

In a dream you are freed of the constraint to be reasonable and levelheaded about whatever concerns you may have about child- birth and motherhood. Your worries can run wild. In fact, the function of your dreams may be to provide an outlet for your inner tension and to help defuse some of your pent-up feelings and fears. And in that sense, even dreams that are better de- scribed as nightmares are positive. Especially if you take the time to replay your dreams and free-associate about the content's possible meaning, dreams can help you come to terms with some of the feelings you may, either consciously or unconsciously, be grappling with.

Increasing forgetfulness, on the other hand, is probably an indication of increased self-preoccupation. As pregnancy draws to an end, many women withdraw into themselves as they get psychologically wrapped up in preparing for both childbirth and motherhood. You may find you can't concentrate for long periods on things that aren't related to pregnancy, for instance, or that you "disengage" from many interests and focus intensely on the upcoming birth and baby. Psychologists don't regard this ten- dency to become "introverted" (which not all women experi- ence) as negative, even if it does lead you to be a bit flaky, distracted, and forgetful. Instead, it's seen as a perfectly healthy way of coping with upcoming changes as well as an indication that you are beginning to get mentally and emotionally prepared for parenthood.

?◆ *Your Life-Style*

THINKING AHEAD ABOUT SOURCES
OF BABY-CARE ADVICE

In addition to family and friends, your pediatrician will be an important source of "trusted advice." In fact, a standard recommendation is that a mother-to-be should choose a pediatrician by her eighth month of pregnancy. Some women actually conduct prenatal interviews of prospective candidates; others simply rely on their obstetrician's recommendation, then meet the doctor after birth. Detailed "how to's" on choosing a pediatrician are included in most childcare guides—guides that, by the way, are likely to be your other main source of "trusted advice."

You'll want to have at least one baby-care manual on hand before your baby's birth (don't be surprised if, in the months after birth, you find you accumulate a veritable library of childcare volumes). The four guides below cover all the essentials: feeding, sleeping, burping, crying, etc., as well as choosing a pediatrician. But they differ dramatically in format, tone, and philosophy. Allow yourself ample browsing time in the bookstore to determine which is likely to suit you best.

Dr. Spock's Baby and Child Care by Benjamin Spock (New York: Pocket, 1989)
An encyclopedic reference work that tends to be more traditional and "strict" in its prescriptions than the other guides. This is an updated version of the classic that has sold thirty million copies.

Your Baby and Child by Penelope Leach (New York: Alfred A. Knopf, 1989)
A copiously illustrated guide that is quite comprehensive and practical as well as "philosophical" on important child development issues. The author holds very deep, specific beliefs about child-rearing. (Compared to Spock, Leach is more "new age" and believes much more in yielding to a baby's needs.)

What to Expect the First Year by Arlene Eisenberg, Heidi Murkoff, and Sandee E. Hathway (New York: Workman, 1989)

This guide, which has a month-by-month question-and-answer format, is easy to use and read. It has a highly practical bent and is strongest in its "how-to" (diaper, breast-feed, burp) sections.

Parents *Book for Your Baby's First Year* by Maja Bernath (New York: Ballantine, 1983)
The smallest-sized pick, this guide is also quite sensible, sensitive, and practical. It's a good book to get your feet wet with if the other volumes overwhelm you with their weight and scope.

10

MONTH NINE

(36 TO 40 WEEKS)

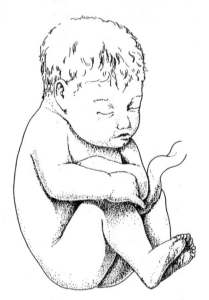

≈ *Your Baby*

WEIGHT: 5½ to 10 pounds
LENGTH: 16½ to 22 inches

The fetus is fast outgrowing the womb; the fit may be so snug that you can actually see the outline of a fist, foot, or the buttocks on your abdomen. In the last week or two, the fetus is likely to move into the best position for birth—facing down, head locked into the ring of pelvic bones. Only a small percentage of fetuses (3 to 4 percent) don't present themselves headfirst for birth, but assume a buttocks-first or breech position instead (see pp. 189–93).

🎵 *Your Body*

MEDICAL INTERVENTIONS IN LABOR AND DELIVERY

I was tempted to title this section "Everything You *Never* Wanted to Know about Childbirth and Were Afraid to Ask." That's because everyone longs for a storybook-perfect childbirth: who wants a cesarean section or an episiotomy? And I know that, before the birth of my baby, the standard advice, "How you bring the baby out is unimportant, it's the end result [a healthy baby] that's essential," was of no great comfort.

Yet the fact remains that medical interventions are sometimes necessary in labor and delivery. And it's important to educate yourself about these procedures; then if you do have to go through one, you'll understand why it's important and what's involved.

Episiotomy (a one- to three-inch-long incision to enlarge the vaginal opening). During my pregnancy I became queasy and weak-kneed every time I came across an illustration (like the one here) of where episiotomy incisions are made. In fact, my dread of having an episiotomy bordered on obsessive. And when I spoke to my obstetrician about having one, I got the answer that the majority of doctors give: "I simply can't say now whether an episiotomy will be necessary or not, although most first-time mothers do need one."

What happened is a scenario experienced by the majority of first-time mothers. After my baby crowned, my doctor said, "Janis, I have to do an episiotomy or else you'll tear." At that point I simply didn't care; besides, what kind of position was I in to object?

If you detect a certain fatalism in my account, you're right. But it's not unwarranted: as many as 90 percent of all first-time mothers who deliver under the care of an obstetrician are given an episiotomy. I think it's fair to say, in fact, that if your doctor does not profess a strong commitment to trying to avoid an episiotomy your chances of having one are quite high. Here are the reasons obstetricians give for performing episiotomies:

• They prevent ragged tears, which are thought to be harder to repair and to take longer to heal than a straight incision.

• They prevent genital prolapse—they help keep the vaginal musculature from overstretching and from subsequently weakening.

• They prevent deep rips into the rectum.

• They prevent potential injury to the fetal head that could be caused by vigorous pushing through the vaginal opening.

The evidence substantiating these claims is, at best, extremely conflicting. For every study that supports them, it appears there is another that refutes them. In other words, whether a woman experiencing a normal labor and delivery actually fares better (i.e., heals faster, has less postpartum pain, etc.) with an episiotomy versus some tearing is highly debatable.

There are certain special situations, though, in which there is clear medical evidence supporting the need for an episiotomy. When forceps are needed in a delivery, when a baby is breech, and/or when a baby is quite large, delivery is much safer (for the baby) when an episiotomy is performed.

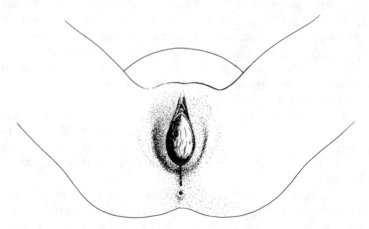

The broken bar shows where the most common type of episiotomy incision is made. In general, a local anesthetic is not needed prior to the cut since the area is effectively numbed by the baby's head pressing on the pelvic-floor muscles. For the stitching afterward, though, a local anesthetic is usually injected. Self-dissolving, self-absorbable sutures are used, so there's nothing to remove later.

In the final analysis, the decision of whether to have an episiotomy is not really yours to make. Only immediately prior to birth can your caregiver determine whether you'll need one; at that point, you simply must be willing to trust his or her judgment. However, by talking with your caregiver before labor, you can at least get an idea of what his or her philosophy is regarding episiotomies. Ask questions: Do you believe in performing episiotomies routinely? Do you perform them on most first-time mothers? What factors go into your decision to perform one? What do you think about the conflicting evidence for and against episiotomies? Do you believe in using massage to relax the vaginal opening as the baby comes down as a potential alternative to an episiotomy? By discussing these things you'll get a good idea of what to expect on your delivery day.

A personal footnote: I was lucky. I didn't find the procedure painful and, unlike some women who find the area is extremely painful postpartum, I only experienced some minor soreness in the weeks afterward. My fears, in other words, were far worse than the reality.

Forceps delivery (forceps, which look like long tongs, grasp the baby's head, then help guide it through the birth canal). Forceps are used most commonly when 1) the mother is too exhausted to effectively push; 2) the mother is unable to bear down well because she is still feeling the effects of painkilling drugs; and/or 3) the baby appears to be in distress and so the fastest delivery possible seems to be important.

Most forceps deliveries are "outlet," meaning the baby's head has already crowned when the forceps are applied, or "low," in which the baby has descended quite far down the birth canal but hasn't crowned when forceps are used. These situations require a local anesthetic and, in most cases, an episiotomy. There are two controversial issues surrounding the use of low or outlet forceps. First, while some studies suggest that their use is quite safe, other data seem to suggest that their use slightly increases the risk of infant death and neurological impairment. Secondly, although there are instances when forceps are clearly needed and, as such, are lifesaving, some physicians still use forceps simply to speed up a slow delivery, which a growing number of experts feel is unnecessarily risky, since delivery is likely to happen naturally given a little patience.

In rarer instances, a forceps delivery is "mid-forceps." In these cases, the head is in the pelvis but hasn't descended very far. This is a riskier procedure and requires regional anesthesia (usually an epidural, spinal, or saddle block) to ensure that the pelvic-floor muscles are fully relaxed, catheterization to empty the bladder, and an extensive episiotomy. Today most doctors opt to perform a cesarean section rather than attempt a mid-forceps delivery.

Almost all forceps deliveries leave a baby with temporary forceps bruises—black-and-blue marks in the temple region which usually fade within a week or so.

An alternative to forceps that you may have heard of is the vacuum extractor. This device sucks the baby's scalp tightly to a cup, then pulls the baby down and through the birth canal. It leaves the baby with a raised "suction" cap at the top of the head for a week after birth. Although some studies suggest that vacuum extraction is less traumatic (for mother and baby), its use has not, to a significant degree, caught on yet in the U.S. (it's popular in Europe).

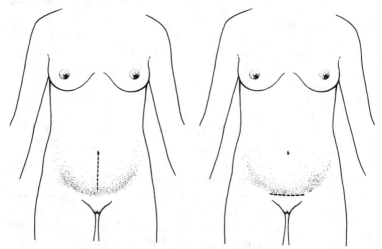

For a cesarean birth, a horizontal incision (right) in the abdominal wall and uterus is usually made. The vertical incision (left) is used only in rare emergencies.

Cesarean birth (delivery of the baby through an incision in the abdomen and uterus). I thought a lot about surgical birth before my labor and delivery, since I knew there was always the chance that I might need one (given that about one out of every four deliveries in the U.S. is by cesarean). Most of the time I would get panicked thinking about the possibility of a cesarean since I desperately wanted a natural birth, and just about everything, from getting anesthesia to coping with surgical pain, scared me. Still, I forced myself to read about cesareans, primarily because I felt that the more I faced my fears, the less likely I would be to feel overwhelmed and confused if I ended up needing one. Although I knew I would be disappointed no matter how much I prepared myself, I did find some comfort in the knowledge that, despite so much press about "unnecessary cesareans," the majority of first-time c-sections *are* needed. They clearly serve to save lives. Also, I forced myself to keep remembering that a cesarean isn't a personal "failure." It's not a character fault, in other words, if you can't give birth vaginally. (For more on the emotional impact of a cesarean delivery, see p. 225.)

Why Cesareans Are Performed

There are a variety of factors that can indicate a cesarean delivery may be safest. They include:

• Malpresentation. Babies who present shoulders, face, or brow first almost always need to be delivered via cesarean; some breech babies (babies who present themselves buttocks first) need to be delivered by c-section.

• Placenta previa. In placenta previa, the placenta, which is normally positioned at the top of the uterus, lies low and blocks the baby's means of egress. This condition is diagnosed before labor, so a woman knows in advance that she must have a c-section.

• Genital herpes. If a herpes infection is active at the time of labor, a cesarean prevents the baby from becoming infected as it passes through the birth canal. However, if testing reveals the infection is dormant, a vaginal delivery is safe.

• Uterine fibroids or tumors. In some cases, these block the vaginal outlet, making a cesarean necessary.

• Cephalopelvic disproportion (CPD). This means that the baby's head is too big to pass through the pelvic outlet. In many cases, CPD isn't diagnosed until after labor has begun.

• Fetal distress. This is one of the more controversial indicators of the need for a cesarean, since definition and management of fetal distress vary widely. However, if a diagnosis of fetal distress that was made on the basis of an electronic fetal monitor reading is confirmed with "fetal scalp sampling," it is a clear indication that there is a real need to get the baby delivered as quickly as possible. Fetal scalp sampling is a technique in which a thin wire is threaded through the cervical opening to obtain a blood sample from the baby's scalp; this sample is then quickly analyzed to see if the baby is being deprived of oxygen.

• Failure to progress. Whether it makes good medical sense to intervene with a cesarean when labor is long, difficult, and slow is a hotly debated subject. Some doctors adhere to labor "timetables": if a woman is greatly "off-schedule" and her labor is unusually sluggish, they are apt to resort to the use of the labor-inducing drug Pitocin (see p. 148), and if that doesn't speed things up effectively, they begin entertaining the idea of a cesarean. Critics of this timetable view feel it simply reveals a lack of patience with the labor process and argue that there is a huge variation in how labors progress—as long as mother and baby don't seem endangered, one should wait and not intervene.

How a Cesarean Is Done

A cesarean takes about one hour, from the administration of anesthesia to the repair of the incision site. If it's not an emergency, more and more hospitals will allow your partner to be present and will allow you to hold and nurse the baby immediately after birth. A cesarean requires the following steps:

1. An IV is inserted into your arm to allow you to receive fluids during the procedure.

2. Your lower abdomen is washed; your pubic hair may be shaved. If general anesthesia will be used, you'll be asleep for the birth; otherwise, most women opt for epidural anesthesia (see p.

161–63), which numbs you from the waist down and allows you to be awake for the delivery.

4. A catheter is inserted into your bladder to keep it empty during surgery.

5. Your doctor makes an incision, first into your abdominal wall, then into your uterus. In extremely rare emergencies, the abdominal and uterine incisions will be vertical (called a midline or classic incision). The advantage of this type of incision is that it can be done quickly; the disadvantage is that there is an increased risk of infection and hemorrhage and of rupture during subsequent deliveries (meaning your next pregnancy would need to be by cesarean, too). In most cases, both the incision in your skin and your uterus is horizontal or transverse, near your pubic hairline. Horizontal incisions require more surgical skill and time to do, but you lose less blood, have a lower risk of infection and hemorrhage, little or no risk of uterine rupture during a subsequent vaginal delivery, and the skin scar is far less visible.

6. The baby is delivered through the incision.

7. The placenta is delivered.

8. The incision is stitched closed.

Postoperative Care

An IV and urinary catheter are usually maintained for at least twenty-four hours after delivery. After about six to eight hours, you should be able to get up and move about; in fact, walking is encouraged because it helps reduce intestinal gas and keeps your lungs from filling with mucus. You'll probably want to hold your incision site, since it may feel very vulnerable and liable to open (although it won't). In most cases, you'll stay in the hospital for four to five days.

If Your Baby Isn't "Head Down"

Ninety-five percent of all babies present themselves for birth with their heads down, chins on chest—the position that makes for the safest, easiest vaginal delivery. The remaining 5 percent of babies present themselves in a variety of ways—buttocks first, shoulder first, face first, etc. These positions make for a more

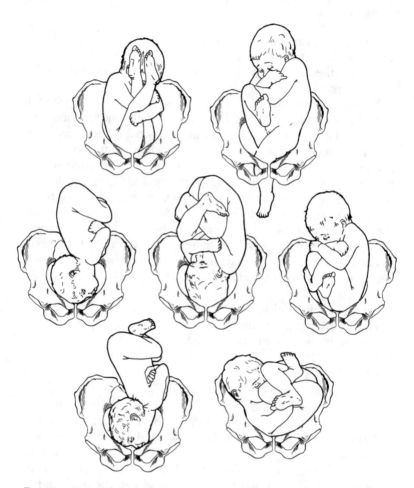

The reason the headfirst or vertex position (at center) is the safest, easiest position for bringing the baby out vaginally has to do with the structure of the fetal head. At the time of birth, the four fetal skull plates are joined by thin, movable membranes. These make it possible for the plates to be squeezed, to overlap, and to change shape so they can fit through the birth canal in a process known as "molding." Other ways baby may "present" for birth, starting from the top left and moving clockwise: frank breech—a vaginal delivery is sometimes possible with this position; footling breech—when one or both feet present themselves at the birth canal, a vaginal delivery is thought to be too risky; complete breech—when in this lotus position, cesarean delivery is merited; shoulder presentation—also called a transverse lie, a cesarean delivery is required; face presentation—it is sometimes possible to coax the fetus to flex his head and tuck it under before birth, but otherwise a cesarean delivery is needed; and brow presentation—only one in every two thousand deliveries involve this position, which requires a cesarean delivery.

difficult labor for several reasons. First, the top of a baby's head is the most effective "dilating wedge," meaning it pushes down on the cervix and forces it open better than other body parts. So when the baby's head is not the presenting part, contractions tend to be weak and the cervix tends to dilate slowly. In fact, if a malpresentation hasn't been diagnosed before labor (which it usually is, since a doctor can feel the baby's position through the abdomen), a prolonged labor will alert doctors that there might be a presentation problem.

Babies who aren't in a head-down position can be tricky to deliver vaginally. Since the head is the largest, hardest body part, when it emerges first, the rest of the baby's body slips out easily. But in the reverse situation, there's the risk that the head might get stuck or have difficulty making its way through the birth canal after the body is born. Also, because the head isn't down, it may not mold properly, which can cause hemorrhaging. Another potential complication is that the umbilical cord may prolapse—it may get compressed when the body emerges first, thus cutting down or even cutting off the baby's supply of oxygen. Finally, in some positions, the baby's shoulder and collarbones may fracture if delivered vaginally.

What causes malpresentation? The reasons aren't fully understood, although the problem does seem to be more likely to occur if a mother:

- has an abnormally shaped uterus
- is pregnant with twins or more
- has the condition of placenta previa
- has had several children
- has an unusually narrow pelvis
- has uterine fibroids

or if a baby:

- is premature
- is underweight (under five and a half pounds)
- has a birth defect

In general, though, the majority of malpresenting babies are perfectly healthy and normal—they simply pose special challenges and demand special consideration when it comes to delivery.

Breech presentation. The word breech means "the hind end of the body." So, obviously, a baby in the breech position is buttocks first. There are three variations on this position: a frank breech, in which the legs are fully extended up over the abdomen; a complete breech, in which the legs are crossed, knees hugged to the chest; and a footling breech, in which one or both feet tend down toward the birth canal (see illustration).

In the case of a complete or footling breech, a cesarean delivery is merited since the risk of trauma is simply too great to try a vaginal delivery. But in the case of frank breech presentation, which is the most common position, a vaginal delivery may be safe if:

• the baby is over three and a half pounds but under eight and a half (this can be roughly estimated using ultrasound)
• the mother's pelvis appears to be big enough to accommodate the baby
• labor progresses steadily
• the baby appears to tolerate labor well
• all the personnel and facilities are immediately at hand in the event that an emergency cesarean delivery is necessary. (In other words, a breech baby shouldn't be delivered vaginally in a nonhospital setting.)

In some cases, it's possible to coax a breech baby to turn prior to birth with a massage technique called external version. Using ultrasound to locate the position of the various body parts, a doctor gently places his or her hands on your abdomen and attempts to manipulate the baby into a headfirst position. This is usually done at thirty-seven or thirty-eight weeks. In some cases, the mother is given a drug prior to the procedure to relax her uterus.

Not all breech babies are candidates for this technique, but when it is used it has a high rate of success. Unfortunately, the baby often spontaneously turns back into the breech position afterward. In some cases, too, a fetus doesn't tolerate massage efforts well, which is why the fetal heartbeat is monitored closely during and after the procedure. If any distress is detected, version attempts are immediately stopped.

Shoulder presentation (transverse lie). The shoulder is usually the body part that enters the vagina first when a baby lies horizontally in the womb during labor. In this situation, a vaginal delivery can be fatal to the fetus; a cesarean delivery is the only safe choice. Luckily, only one out of every three hundred to four hundred deliveries involve this position.

Face and brow presentation. When the baby's head is thrown back rather than tucked under, either the face or the eyebrows will be the presenting part. This situation is quite rare—face presentation occurs in approximately 1 in 250 deliveries; brow presentation, 1 in 2000 deliveries. If it's diagnosed very early in labor, it is sometimes possible to get the baby to flex his or her head via external manipulation. However, in most cases, a cesarean delivery is believed to be the safest option.

❧ Your Doctor Appointment

WHEN BABY IS LATE

Deciding what to do when a pregnancy extends two weeks beyond a woman's due date can be one of the more difficult decisions an obstetrician must make. Is it safe to keep waiting? Should labor be induced? Or is it wisest to do a cesarean? The answers to these questions are unclear since no study results are yet available regarding the management and outcome of postterm pregnancy (there is a study under way, sponsored by the federal government, but the results won't be in for several more years).

There are three potential complications in simply waiting for labor to begin naturally: 1. The placenta may start to age and stop delivering adequate amounts of food and oxygen. 2. The baby may become overlarge and extremely difficult to deliver. 3. The umbilical cord may get compressed, cutting off the baby's supply of food and oxygen, and the uterus become too over-crowded. These possibilities put post-mature babies at increased risk of brain damage and, even, death.

But the alternative approaches—inducing labor or electing to deliver by cesarean—carry risks, too. The biggest risk is that a doctor may end up intervening in a pregnancy that is not really past term. Frequently, a woman's due date is miscalculated (which is easy to do, for instance, if a woman isn't sure about the date of her last period), so the baby is really not overdue. Also, it may be that it is natural for some babies to stay in utero longer than others; some babies may simply take less time, others more, to mature.

Inducing labor is also extremely difficult if the cervix hasn't displayed signs of readiness—i.e., when it hasn't begun to efface and dilate on its own. Labor induced under these cirumstances increases the risk that a woman will experience an abnormal labor and/or uterine rupture. Also, in many cases, the induction will not be effective, meaning a woman may end up enduring hours and hours of labor only to end up needing a cesarean.

Tests to Check Up on the Postdate Fetus

Luckily, there are three tests that can at least help an obstetrician determine whether the postdate fetus is at risk. In fact, after you pass forty-one weeks in your pregnancy, your doctor may want to perform the following tests twice weekly:

• The nonstress test (NST). This measures whether the fetus's heart rate accelerates with movement; if it does, it's a sign that all is still well. The test takes about forty minutes; you recline, while an ultrasound transducer or "wand" that is placed on your abdomen picks up the fetal heart rate.
• Biophysical profile. Usually done in conjunction with the NST, this ultrasound exam attempts to assess if your baby's size is in healthy proportion to the amount of amniotic fluid present in the uterus.
• Contraction stress test (CST). This assesses how the fetus's heart rate responds to uterine contractions. If the fetus is getting enough oxygen, the heart rate won't slow in reaction to con-

tractions. Standard electronic fetal monitoring equipment is used for this test, which is performed while you recline.

As long as these tests show that the fetus is thriving, some doctors are willing to wait "indefinitely" for labor to begin naturally. Other doctors, though, have "personal" cutoff dates, such as forty-one or forty-four weeks, when they feel it's time to induce labor or deliver via cesarean. Before opting for this kind of non-emergency intervention, however, you may want to try to coax labor to begin by stimulating your nipples frequently (every five or ten minutes, for one to two minutes at a time) and by walking around and keeping active as much as possible. As long as the fetus seems healthy, your doctor is likely to be willing to wait a few more days while you give these "do-it-yourself" tactics a try.

‹ê Your Diet

THINKING AHEAD ABOUT POSTPARTUM DINING

One thing that having a baby will definitely change is the way you plan dinner. If you almost always eat out now, for example, chances are you won't want to drag your newborn to restaurants every night, and you'll find yourself eating home more. On the other hand, before I gave birth, I tried new recipes all the time, thought nothing of making special trips to out-of-the-way specialty food stores, and found it "no sweat" to entertain large numbers of guests, even last-minute ones. Now, I'm not inclined to devote lots of time to dinner preparation because it robs me of leisure time with my baby. On a less altruistic note, I find it hard to put together anything that requires precise timing since my daughter invariably clamors for me at *the* crucial moment. Also, my daughter, like many babies, for some uncanny reason, gets her most demanding at precisely the moment I sit down to eat—and I know I find this much less frustrating when I haven't fussed a great deal to get dinner on the table.

Yet I haven't given up eating well (something that is especially important for keeping healthy postpartum and for breast-feeding), cooking, or entertaining—I've just streamlined things dramatically so everything is much, much simpler. I reject any recipe that has too many complicated steps or requires split-second timing. Just about everything I make can be prepared in advance; that way, I can do my preparing during the baby's nap time. And I almost never make dessert—I ask guests to bring it. I also triple recipes and freeze the extra batches now (my freezer, pre-baby, was used exclusively for ice cubes and ice cream).

That the arrival of a baby can cause dramatic changes in the dinner hour was one of those things I wish someone had warned me about. Forewarning might have helped me experience fewer frustrating moments as well as helping me figure out much faster which recipes were still "doable."

❧ Your Workout

PRACTICING LABOR POSITIONS

There are several reasons why being in an upright position—kneeling, squatting, standing, or walking around—not only helps you to be more comfortable during labor, but helps to make childbirth easier for you. When in an upright position:

• You take advantage of the force of gravity, which helps enhance the baby's movement down the birth canal.
• The amount of pressure placed on your lower back is decreased, thus easing back pain.
• Blood flow to the uterus is increased, which increases the strength of contractions, leading to a shorter labor.
• You have better leverage for pushing and you can generate stronger, more efficient bearing-down efforts.

Lying immobile, flat on your back, is not only one of the least comfortable positions you could assume during labor, but it can actually make labor and delivery longer and harder (for example, in a recent study of the deliveries of four hundred women conducted in England, women who assumed the traditional inclined position had to push ten minutes longer in second-stage labor and had a 6 percent higher rate of forceps delivery than women who adopted a modified squatting position).

The best way to ensure you will be able to move about freely

A stable bureau top or sturdy chair can lend support as you work through contractions. Whenever you feel tired or uncomfortable in a position, be sure to switch to another.

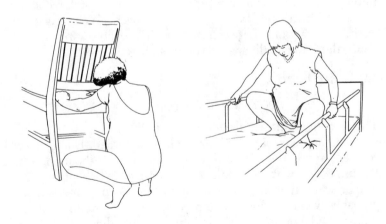

To stretch and strengthen calf and thigh muscles, practice the squatting position now; during labor, only squat during contractions, to avoid straining your muscles.

during labor is to labor at home as long as possible. Laboring in a hospital often requires you to lie in bed, for long stretches, for exams, fetal monitoring, etc.

Being able to actually deliver your baby in a squatting position is a rarity in this country, although some hospitals now have birthing chairs (which support a woman in a squatting position during delivery). Most obstetricians and even certified nurse-midwives, however, prefer you to be in bed during second-stage labor (the pushing stage) and to recline during the final moments of delivery, since that allows them to best see what is happening. However, until your baby's head crowns (the top of his or her head appears at the vaginal opening), you may be able to assume a half sitting or semi-squatting position in your hospital bed to enhance your pushing efforts.

The illustrations on p. 197 show you a few of the positions you may want to try out during labor to make yourself more comfortable. The squatting positions, in particular, are ones you may want to practice now, since they are positions you, in all likelihood, don't normally get into while working, exercising, cleaning, etc. You should be able to squat easily for two to three minutes, about the time it takes you to feel a contraction coming on, to work through it, and then to recover. You'll only squat during contractions. Between them you'll probably want to lie on your side, stand, walk around, or kneel with support.

⋩ *Your Feelings*

COPING WITH CHILDBIRTH FEARS

The starting point for dealing with childbirth fears is to accept that your apprehension can't be totally vanquished. Don't expect yourself, in other words, to be completely fearless about entering the unknown: why shouldn't you be a bit scared about stepping into an event that involves pain and is unpredictable? Also, you probably won't be able to stop yourself from dwelling on the impending labor and delivery. So rather than drain your energy by trying to deny or avoid your fears, it makes sense to try to confront them in a constructive way.

Let's say, for example, that one of your big fears is having a cesarean section. If you deal with this by avoiding the subject—

by refusing to educate yourself about what's involved in a c-section—you run the risk of feeling helpless and scared during the procedure, then of being deeply resentful and disappointed postpartum. On the other hand, if you take control of your fear by facing it and learning everything you can about cesareans, how they're done, how they're sometimes lifesaving, you can come away from the experience feeling brave and strong about having had to accept the decision to deliver by cesarean.

Other common fears include:

Fear of Not Being Able to Deliver Without Anesthesia

To keep in mind: A deep-seated desire to withstand childbirth pain without resorting to anesthesia will, first of all, go a long way toward helping you handle it unassisted. However, it's important to resist forming this equation in your mind: if I ask for a painkiller, it means that I am weak and I "fail." If you set up childbirth as a test of your machisma, you risk being deeply disappointed in yourself. Even worse, you may become so preoccupied with your feelings of failure postpartum that you miss out on the joyousness of your baby's birth and first days of life. So it's important to move away from the idea that if you ask for a pain blocker it somehow reflects negatively on your strength and character. Instead, if you accept the fact that you may need anesthesia, there's a much greater chance that, if you end up requesting a painkiller, birth will still be an exhilarating, positive experience for you.

Fear of Pain

To keep in mind: If you learn all you can about pain-relief options, you'll be reassured that you'll be able to receive help quickly if you want it. Also, it helps to remember that labor pains are not long, drawn out, and unremitting. Instead, contraction pains usually last under one and a half minutes, and when a contraction ends, you experience virtually no pain at all until the next contraction begins. You get respite from the pain, in other words. It's not unceasing and constant.

Fear of Medical Procedures

To keep in mind: Again, the key is to educate yourself, so at least you won't panic if you need a "dreaded" medical procedure. Also, what you imagine about a procedure ahead of time can be much worse than the reality in some cases. An episiotomy (a procedure particularly dreaded by most women), for example, sounds awful and scary, like something to be avoided at all costs. But if the time comes when you need one, you probably won't think twice about consenting and you won't feel the procedure being performed at all.

Fear of How You'll Act and React

Childbirth educators sometimes mistakenly lead women to believe that they may somehow undergo a Dr. Jekyll-and-Mr. Hyde–like personality transformation during labor. But the idea these instructors really intend to convey is that certain character traits may become exaggerated during labor. For example, there's a good chance you will verbally abuse your coach during transition if you tend to lash out in everyday life. In the same way, if you're not prone to hysteria, it's unlikely you'll become hysterical during labor. In other words, you're unlikely to behave in a manner that is totally foreign to your nature. In fact, if you can honestly look at how you act in stressful situations, you'll have a good preview of how you're likely to behave during labor.

In the end, the more you're able to accept that you can't possibly know how events will unfold, the more at peace you'll be with whatever scenario actually occurs. Also, the more knowledge you have about the things that scare you, the more in charge and confident you'll feel, no matter what happens.

❧ Your Life-Style

WHAT TO PACK FOR THE HOSPITAL

Common advice is not to pack money, the reason being that it might get stolen. Yet I desperately wished I had $10 or $20 hidden somewhere in my luggage because without it I couldn't a) buy the morning newspaper; b) pay to have the television turned on, and c) pay for photographs to be taken in the nursery. Other things I wished I had packed: pen and paper, a telephone credit card (needed for making long distance calls, which I had to make collect since I didn't have a card), the phone number of my health insurance carrier (which I needed to contact within three days of giving birth in order to receive full benefits), and lots of snacks, such as boxed cookies, crackers, and dried fruits (for munching in the middle of the night, when you're likely to be awake, especially if you're nursing). In addition, you'll want to bring the following essentials:

- Nightgown
- Robe
- Slippers
- Underwear
- Bras
- Nursing pads
- Set of clothes to leave the hospital in
- Toothbrush
- Toothpaste
- Shampoo
- Hairbrush
- Soap
- Sanitary napkins
- Face and hand cream
- Cosmetics
- Set of clothes to bring baby home in (an undershirt, a one-piece "stretchie," booties, a cap, and a receiving blanket)
- Infant nail scissors (in most nurseries, staff won't cut a newborn's fingernails, which can be quite long at birth and with which an infant can easily scratch himself or herself)
- Baby-care guide—if you haven't been able to muster up a lot of interest in these books prior to delivery, you'll probably be surprised at how you want to devour them postpartum. Also bring this book.

LABOR LUGGAGE

During labor you may want to have quick access to these items:

• Mouthwash (if your labor is long and/or you vomit during labor, you'll want to freshen your mouth/breath)
• Lip balm (since your lips can get parched during a long labor)
• Warm socks (some women find their feet get unusually cold)
• Hair tie (if your hair is long, you'll want it out of your face)
• Snacks—for you after delivery and for your coach during labor

11

MONTH TEN
(POSTPARTUM)

❧ Your Baby

GETTING TO KNOW YOUR NEWBORN

If you didn't learn the sex of your baby during pregnancy, your first question after birth is likely to be, "What is it?" And fast on the heels of that query will be, "Is everything okay?" The answer to this question will largely be supplied by how your newborn scores on the Apgar test, a test designed by the late Virginia Apgar, M.D., professor of anesthesiology at Columbia University. The Apgar, which is usually performed by a delivery-room nurse, is a measurement of these five vital signs:

- A: appearance
- P: pulse
- G: grimace (i.e., reflexes)
- A: activity
- R: respiration

Each of these five functions is given a score of 0, 1 or 2. For example, in rating a baby's cry as an indication of respiratory strength, a fierce, hearty cry will be given a 2, a weak cry a 1, and no cry, a 0. A "perfect" Apgar score is a 10; the lowest is a 0.

Apgar ratings are usually performed twice, one minute after birth, then again five minutes after birth. That's why ratings are usually quoted as two numbers. A baby's Apgar will be said to be a "8–9," for example. The score at the five-minute mark is thought to be especially reflective of a baby's immediate general condition; a score of seven or higher is considered normal and healthy, while lower scores indicate that the baby needs special attention and, possibly, medical assistance. It's important to keep in mind, though, that your baby's Apgar doesn't necessarily predict *long-term* health and development—it just tells you whether your baby needs special care at birth.

Your Newborn's Appearance

As you get to know your infant in the first hours and days after birth, you may be surprised by some of these perfectly normal aspects of his or her appearance:

• Blue fingers and toes—which may feel cold to the touch, too. Within a day or two, when circulation fully "revs up," your baby's extremities will turn pink like the rest of the body.

• Dry, flaky skin. This is simply some residue from the vernix caseosa, the greasy coating that protected the baby in utero.

• Long body hair. These remnants of lanugo, the long, silky hair the baby grew for insulation purposes in the uterus, fall out within a few weeks.

• Big head. Newborns are born out of proportion: body-wise, the size of their various body parts will normalize within the first few months of life.

• Red spots or blotches, especially on the face. What causes these isn't known, but they disappear in a few weeks.

• Tiny whitish or yellowish cysts. These spots (called milia) on the cheeks, nose, and chin clear up on their own in a few weeks.

• Bloodshot eyes. Specks of blood in the whites of the eyes are hemorrhages caused by pressure and squeezing during delivery. They clear up in a week or two.

• Blister on the upper lip. Called a nursing blister, it's caused by vigorous sucking. It may shed and reemerge during the first month or two.

• Bowed legs. Turned-in feet are also normal until a baby

learns to walk. Breech babies may have legs and feet that turn outward—this is also normal and will correct itself when walking begins.

• Vaginal discharge or bleeding. Newborn girls often have something akin to a period in the first days of life; this is caused by high levels of circulating maternal hormones. Once your hormones clear from her system, which takes a few days, these symptoms will disappear.

• "Leaky" breasts. Both male and female babies may have enlarged breasts that discharge a milklike substance until maternal hormones clear from their system, usually within a few days after birth.

• Enlarged genitals. Newborn boys and girls may have swollen-looking genitals for several months after birth.

❧ WHEN YOUR BABY HAS JAUNDICE ❧

Jaundice is quite common among babies; an estimated 25 to 50 percent of all normal newborns exhibit signs of it, while an even higher percentage of low-birth-weight and premature babies have symptoms. The chances of a baby's being jaundiced may be slightly increased, too, if a mother has epidural anesthesia and/or Pitocin to induce or speed up labor.

The characteristic features of jaundice, a yellowing of the skin and the whites of the eyes, is caused by an excess of bilirubin in the blood. Bilirubin is a natural by-product of the breakdown of "used" or dead red blood cells; newborns tend to produce a great amount of it because they shed lots of red blood cells in the first few weeks of life (a baby needs more red blood cells in utero than he or she needs after birth). Normally, this bilirubin is metabolized by the liver, with bacterial enzymes in the intestines further helping to break it down so it can be excreted in the feces. But often a baby's liver is too immature and his or her intestinal enzymes are still too inactive to process the bilirubin fast enough, so it builds up in the blood and, between the second and fifth day of life, causes what is known as "physiologic" jaundice.

Physiologic jaundice is often mild and harmless, requiring no treatment. Bilirubin buildup usually peaks, approximately, on the third day after birth, then begins to clear up on its own. If it doesn't clear up and becomes severe, though, the buildup of bilirubin can lead to damage of brain and nerve tissues. In addition, physiologic jaundice can be difficult to distinguish from "pathological" jaundice, a relatively rare condition that can be caused by infection, disease, an internal defect, or blood incompatibility between mother and baby. If left untreated, it also can cause brain damage.

Treating jaundice. Exactly when and if a jaundiced baby needs to be treated often depends on the baby's size, general condition, and the rate at which his or her bilirubin numbers are rising. In addition, there are different philosophies about when to order treatment; some doctors are of the "better safe than sorry" school, while others have a more "wait and see" attitude. But, in general, these are how bilirubin numbers are interpreted: seventy-two to ninety-six hours after birth, bilirubin levels under twelve milligrams are usually considered safe, numbers between twelve to eighteen milligrams, depending on the baby's size, may demand either close monitoring or immediate treatment; levels above twenty milligrams almost always indicate the need for treatment, even for normal-weight, full-term babies.

The most common treatment for jaundice is phototherapy, in which artificial light is used to help break down and decompose the bilirubin (which is photosensitive). The baby, who is usually naked except for a diaper, with his or her eyes well shielded, is placed in an incubator that is brightly illuminated by fluorescent lights. Except for feedings, the baby stays under the lights continuously until his or her bilirubin levels drop. Only very severe cases of pathologic jaundice are treated with blood transfusions (in which the baby's bilirubin-loaded blood is replaced with donor blood).

Phototherapy is simple and effective, but it can have side effects; when under the lights for several days, babies tend to become lethargic, feed poorly, and may develop diarrhea, skin rashes, and a vitamin B-2 deficiency. There's a "side effect" for parents too, since phototherapy creates a highly stressful situation. Phototherapy usually begins on precisely the day a mother is to be discharged from the hospital. That means she must leave the hospital without her baby. If she plans to nurse she must return every few hours for feedings and/or pump her breasts in between. Still, when phototherapy is unquestionably indicated, the risk of allowing bilirubin levels to rise unchecked far outweighs these other risks and drawbacks.

What you can do. The moment you learn your baby may be at risk for jaundice, there are steps you can take that may help stop the rise in bilirubin. First, breast-feed your baby as often as possible and for as long as possible. Your pre-milk or colostrum is a natural laxative, and the more a baby eliminates, the more bilirubin he or she excretes. In the typical hospital routine, your baby will only be brought to your room to be breast-fed every three or four hours. If that's the case, try going to the nursery to feed your baby in between scheduled feedings. If you encounter resistance—if the nursery attendants try to limit your access to your baby to scheduled times, for instance—get your pediatrician to intervene in your behalf.

Secondly, expose your baby's skin to sunlight as much as possible. Undress your baby and sit with him or her by a window where there is direct sunlight (the window should be closed to avoid the possibility of sunburn). This will have essentially the same beneficial effects as phototherapy, which is really nothing more than an artificial substitute for sunshine.

What if there is no sun on the days you are in the hospital? Sitting with your baby under a bright fluorescent light may help. Be sure to shield your baby's eyes, by either lightly placing your hand or a lightweight cloth over his or her eyes.

Most hospitals are unaccustomed to a mother being an "activist" when faced with the possible diagnosis of jaundice. The main thing to watch out for are doctors and nurses who try to sabotage your efforts by suggesting that you can't possibly make a difference. It will be easier to stand your ground if you keep these facts in mind: 1) numerous studies have established that early, frequent breast-feeding helps flush out bilirubin; 2) water, sugar or glucose water, and supplementary formula—things many nurses may urge you to give your baby—have not been shown to be of any value in clearing up jaundice. Your pre-milk or colostrum has a unique composition that speeds your baby's passage of bilirubin-laden stools; and 3) phototherapy mimics sunshine—it was, in fact, developed in response to the discovery that sunlight is beneficial in clearing up jaundice. So don't let anyone convince you that sitting with your baby in a sunny window is silly or unlikely to do good.

There is, of course, the possibility that despite your best efforts, your baby may still need to undergo phototherapy. If this is the case, ask about the possibility of home phototherapy—although the practice is still rare, some hospitals actually have portable light setups that can be used at home.

Although it is scary and stressful to have your baby undergoing phototherapy, it helps to remember that the situation won't last forever and it is serving the purpose of preventing permanent brain damage. It's best for you and your baby if you can spend as much time as possible in the nursery during phototherapy. Your touch will provide your baby with comfort, and even if you aren't breast-feeding, taking part in bottle feedings will help you to get to know your baby better (and help your baby to get to know you).

?● *Your Body*

WHAT HAPPENS AFTER BIRTH?

Your body begins to change immediately after birth and it keeps changing over the next several months. A common rule of thumb is "nine months to get there, nine months to get back," although most women take much less time to fully recover and get back to "normal." Here, then, is a rundown of the physical aftereffects you may experience in the first postpartum hours and days, as well as in the following weeks and months.

The shakes. Immediately following delivery some women are seized with chills and shake uncontrollably. It's not known why this happens; perhaps it's a response to the sudden, dramatic weight loss or it may be a sort of "quick cooling" reaction after the heavy exertion of pushing. These shakes rarely last longer than the time you spend in the recovery room, where you should ask for a warm blanket.

After-pains. The uterus must keep contracting after delivery in order to return to its prepregnancy size (which it does within six weeks). And these uterine contractions often cause cramping sensations, especially during the first two postpartum days. Also, the cramping will be more intense during your first breast-feeding sessions, because breast-feeding stimulates the release of the contraction-triggering hormone oxytocin. If you find afterpains really uncomfortable, a mild analgesic like acetaminophen (Tylenol) will provide some relief. Tylenol, as long as it's without codeine or other added ingredients, appears to be safe to use while breast-feeding.

Vaginal discharge. For at least three to six weeks after delivery, you'll experience a discharge called lochia, which consists of blood, mucus, and bits of uterine lining. For the first three to four days, the discharge tends to be heavy, dark red, and will tend to increase in flow when you stand, walk, and/or breast-feed; for the next two weeks, the lochia will tend to be more pink or reddish brown; for the last one to four weeks, the lochia tends to be thinner, scanter, and more yellow or whitish in color.

Any of the characteristics below may signal the presence of an infection or be an indication that some placental tissue has been retained:

- Discharge that is still profuse and bright red two weeks postpartum
- Lochia that contains large pieces of tissue
- Discharge that has a strong, offensive odor

If you experience any of these symptoms you should contact your doctor.

Episiotomy site soreness. No two episiotomies are alike, which means it's hard to really make generalizations about the healing process. Obviously, though, the more minimal the incision, the less soreness and tenderness you'll experience. But regardless of the extent of your episiotomy, there are two "tools" you should have (which most hospitals supply): 1) a plastic "peri" bottle, with which you can squeeze cool water on your vagina after urinating in lieu of "wiping"; and 2) an inflated plastic ring or "doughnut" to sit on, which ensures no pressure or weight is put on the sutures when you sit.

Other measures that provide comfort:

• Local anesthetic sprays or ointments, which should only be used after the area has been well cleansed. Also, it's important to watch for an allergic reaction, since some women experience itching or get a rash from these sprays.
• An ice pack, which you keep tucked between your legs for fifteen minutes at a time.
• Heat lamp treatment. After your vaginal area has been well cleansed, you lie down while your stitches are exposed to heat from a light bulb for fifteen to twenty minutes at a time. Not only is that soothing, but it stimulates circulation and thus speeds healing.
• Sitz bath. This is essentially a soak in plain warm water. Most hospitals have sitz-bath units that fit over a toilet.
• Mild analgesic, such as acetaminophen (Tylenol)

Hemorrhoids. Very often, hemorrhoids—which are enlarged, distended rectal veins—develop as a result of vigorous pushing during labor. Their size and most of the discomfort they cause generally decreases after the first two or three postpartum days. In addition, most hemorrhoids that developed during pregnancy will disappear completely within a few months.

The treatment for hemorrhoid pain is similar to that for episiotomy soreness: ice compresses, anesthetic sprays, heat lamp treatment, and sitz baths. Also, cold witch-hazel compresses (Tucks) may provide relief.

Night sweats. During the first postpartum week, this profuse perspiration at nighttime may be one of the ways your body gets rid of fluids retained during pregnancy.

Constipation. Bowel sluggishness for the first two or three days is normal. You may also be a bit afraid that defecating will cause pain if you have hemorrhoids or have had an episiotomy. To ensure elimination normalizes by day three or four postpartum, eat plenty of fresh fruits, vegetables, and whole grains; drink lots of liquids, especially water, and keep as active as possible.

Gas pains. Women who have had cesarean births in particular find this to be a problem. Moving around is the best remedy; rocking in a rocking chair and drinking effervescent liquids, such as ginger ale, can help, too.

Dizziness. If you had any kind of anesthesia during labor and delivery, you may feel woozy and weak the first few times you get up.

Incision pain. A cesarean birth is major surgery, and you'll probably receive strong pain medications for at least the first twenty-four hours. After that, you will gradually be switched to lesser-strength pain relievers. You may be able to do without prescription pain medication, although occasionally you may need over-the-counter relievers such as Tylenol, for up to six to eight weeks. If you are breast-feeding, these pain medications can pass through your milk, but they don't seem to pose any long-term health threat to the baby.

Breasts. In the first two postpartum days, you'll probably notice very little change in the appearance of your breasts. Probably the only difference will be that they secrete colostrum, a yellowish pre-milk that contains important disease-fighting antibodies. But by the third or fourth postpartum day, your milk will "come in" and, with that, your breasts will become larger, heavier, harder, and more "veiny." (My milk came in at night, when I was asleep. When I woke up, I was astounded to discover that I suddenly had big breasts). Once your milk comes in, your breasts may feel hot, tingly, and lumpy. This is simply a result of the first filling of your breasts with milk; once breast-feeding is established, these sensations will subside in intensity.

If you don't plan to nurse your baby, the best way to relieve the discomfort of initial engorgement is to wear a tight bra to compress the milk glands and to apply ice packs to your breasts occasionally. You may also want to take pain relievers (however, avoid anti-lactation drugs, since they have been increasingly associated with adverse, major side effects). Engorgement pain will subside in a few days as milk production begins to halt.

Difficulty urinating. You may find it difficult to urinate the first time after delivery since your urethra may be sore and swollen because of pressure put on it during delivery and/or catheterization. You may hold back out of fear that the urine will cause burning in the episiotomy area. But if you don't overcome your reluctance to urinate on your own, catheterization or re-catheterization may be necessary. Drink lots of liquids so you won't be able to avoid voiding. Also, it may help to run water in the sink, to drink something warm beforehand, and/or to pour warm water over your vagina when attempting to urinate for the first time. Generally, once you've managed to urinate that first time, you'll be reassured that it doesn't really hurt and so won't have trouble subsequently.

If, however, you feel a deep, burning sensation when you urinate, and/or you feel an intense urge to urinate, but are only able to pass a few drops, notify your doctor. You may have a urinary tract infection.

Deeply exhausted/achy. Especially if you had a long, difficult labor, you may feel very wiped out, stiff, and sore. This "beat-up" feeling usually begins to fade in a week or two.

Weight loss. The average weight loss at delivery is thirteen to fifteen pounds (although some women lose less and some women drop back to their prepregnancy weight in the first postpartum week). If you're breast-feeding, you should more or less stick to the same diet you ate during pregnancy (see pp. 222–23). But if you're bottle-feeding, you won't need to eat the same volume of food you ate in the past nine months. For many women, cutting down the amount of calories they consume just happens naturally. Their appetite decreases and they "diet" with little overt effort. But if you've always been prone to overeating or to weight gain, or, if you don't seem to be dropping your pounds steadily, you may need to make a conscious effort to cut down. Patience is the watchword here, though: the only way to lose your weight in a healthy manner is to lose it gradually. Drastic diets will leave you fatigued, hungry, and irritable—three things that will make it difficult for you to care for (not to mention enjoy) your new baby.

BREAST-FEEDING TIME

People who have never breast-fed tend to joke, "What's there to learn?" But for most women, nursing doesn't just come "naturally"—it's a skill that takes time and some patience to master. It took me weeks, for instance, to figure out how to nurse while lying down—I simply couldn't find a position that "worked" and was comfortable. It also took me time to accept that breast-feeding for me and my daughter, at least, was not going to be a beatific Madonna and Child–type scenario. My daughter tended to scream and fuss before she settled into eating, which meant my breast flailed in the air for all to see until she latched on (so much for discreet, public breast-feeding!).

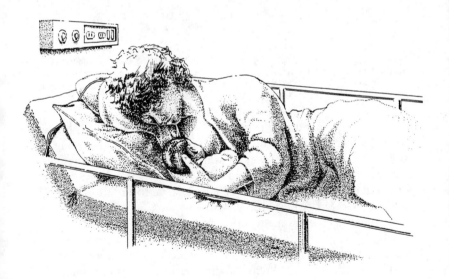

To nurse lying down, prop your head up, using pillows and your arm. Then, with your free arm, draw your baby close to your breast. If necessary, use your hand to guide your nipple and some of the dark skin around it into his or her mouth.

The more comfortable and relaxed you are, the better your "let-down" response—the response that triggers the release of milk from ducts and causes it to flow freely. So especially in the first few weeks, you may want to retire to a quiet room and relax by taking a few deep "cleansing" breaths before each nursing session.

But once your nursing relationship gets established, it is likely to seem like second nature to you. In the meantime, though, there are lots of resources available to help you maneuver through the rough times. Besides advice you can cull from your obstetrician or pediatrician, La Leche League International has a hotline, 1-800-LA-LECHE (9 A.M.–3 P.M. CST) that will give you immediate answers to your breast-feeding questions, will send you brochures about breast-feeding, and will put you in contact with your local La Leche League support group. Below you'll find the basics of breast-feeding outlined. This information comes from the pamphlet "Breastfeeding Problems Can Be Avoided" (published by Health Education Associates [HEA], 8 Jan Sebastian Way, Sandwich, MA 02563; 508-888-8044). If you feel you want to read more, HEA has other booklets on breast-feeding that you can order; your neighborhood bookstore or library is also likely to have at least two or three titles devoted solely to breast-feeding.

Painful sore nipples can be avoided. At first you may have tender nipples or a little discomfort when the baby latches on, but you can definitely avoid painfully sore nipples. Soreness usually comes from improper positioning. So, the secret to avoiding nipple soreness is in proper positioning, rather than in the use of any nipple cream.

1. *Position the baby's mouth properly.* The important thing is to make sure that the baby's mouth does *not* suck on just the nipple. The baby's mouth should be wide open and he should latch on to the darker (areola) skin around the nipple. To do this:

• Have your baby's body up near your breast—not down on the bottom of your lap. A pillow can help.
• Use one hand to cup your breast—your hand makes the shape of the letter C.
• Let your nipple tickle your baby's lips. Wait for him to open his mouth wide.
• Pull your baby's body in toward you and let his wide-open mouth latch onto the darker (areola) skin around your nipple. If you need to, you can use the thumb of your other hand to make a little air space for the baby to breathe.

To see if the position is correct, check to be sure:
—your baby is very close to you—tummy to tummy
—your baby's mouth is well up on the areola skin
• Break suction properly to end the feeding. You can insert your clean little finger into the corner of the baby's mouth.

2. *Use the good, simple breast-care routines that have been proven effective in research.* After each feeding, let your nipples air dry. Leave the flaps of your nursing bra down. Even under a loose-fitting robe, you're still air drying.

Breasts are not dirty and do not need to be washed. During your daily shower, plain water is fine. *Avoid soap and all other drying agents.* As long as you haven't put anything on your nipples, you do not need to do anything to your breasts before you nurse the baby.

So breast care is very simple:

- Take a daily shower or bath with no soap on the nipples.
- Air dry your nipples after nursing.

By keeping breast-care routines simple, each feeding is simple—just pick up the baby and nurse. This is fortunate because then it's easy to nurse often enough in the first few days.

3. Use frequent nursings. There are many advantages to nursing frequently—that is about ten times in twenty-four hours in the first month:

- Your milk will come in sooner and your baby will start to gain weight faster.
- There is less chance of jaundice among babies who nurse often.
- If you nurse often, you are less likely to find your breasts getting overfull or engorged.
- Human milk is very dilute and easy on your baby's kidneys, etc. It is so easy to digest that babies need to nurse very often—every one to three hours. By nursing often, you will be sure that your baby gets enough milk. Babies who nurse only every four hours usually do not make good weight gains.
- If you nurse often—*at least* every two and a half to three hours in the daytime—your baby won't get overly hungry and be too hard on your nipples.

How long should each nursing session last? In the beginning, five to ten minutes total may be a good time to keep in mind. But no one can tell you exactly how long. A sleepy baby needs a little longer than a baby who is a strong nurser.

It's better to watch your beautiful baby—not your clock or watch. In a study in England almost half of the mothers who were told to time their nursings (by the clock) had totally given up breast-feeding by six weeks, although 80 percent of similar mothers who watched their babies were happily breast-feeding. Following the clock is not a good idea!

You can avoid engorgement, too. Engorgement means over-fullness in the breasts. After the milk comes in—around the third day postpartum—women usually feel quite full. This is normal. All the fullness is not milk; there is also some swelling and increased blood supply to the breasts. The swelling will go away by itself by about the tenth day after delivery. *Your breasts will seem flatter because the swelling (not the milk) has gone away.* This *does not mean* that you are losing your milk.

Some women find that the normal fullness turns into a serious case of overfullness. This overfullness leaves the breasts hard, painful, and warm to the touch.

If you're doing the things that keep your nipples from getting painfully sore, you're already doing the things that prevent engorgement. The most important advice is to nurse frequently. When you nurse often, you keep your full breasts from turning into overfull breasts. While in the hospital, ask to have your baby brought to you at night. If your baby is sleepy, wake him or her up. Watch your baby for times when he or she is most alert and use these times for nursings.

If your breasts get too full, the nipples can look flat and it's harder for the baby to grasp on. You may need to gently hand-express a small amount of milk right before the feeding. When the area right under the nipple is softer, it's easier for the baby to latch on. Some women like to hand-express in a nice warm shower.

If you leak, try to look at it as a minor annoyance. Some women never leak milk at all, probably because they have tighter muscles that hold the milk in. Most new mothers leak, some more than others. The bad news is that there is no exercise to tighten the little muscles in the nipple—no way to completely stop the leaking. But the good news is that the leaking tapers off by itself. As time goes by, most women leak less and less. Often women who are nursing a second or third child find that they no longer leak.

What can you do? To stop the flow temporarily, put gentle pressure against the breast. You can cross your arms casually across your chest. At the beginning of a feeding, you probably will leak from the other breast, because the milk naturally flows from both breasts at the same time. You can gently push on the other breast to stop the flow, or you can use a nursing pad.

Nursing pads can also be worn in between feedings. Drugstores sell disposable ones. Pick ones that do not have a plastic liner in them. The plastic might keep your shirt dry but it will prevent air from circulating. It's more important to air dry to prevent sore nipples.

Nursing pads that are made of cloth can be rewashed and save you money. Most women also find them more comfortable.

You may have heard of hard plastic cups or shields that new mothers can wear between feedings. While it might sound logical to wear such cups because they can help keep your clothing dry, it is not a good idea. By putting constant pressure on the area around the nipples, the cups actually encourage more leaking. That pressure is something like the pressure of a baby's jaws and it tells the woman's body that milk should come out. So avoid wearing any hard plastic cups or shields between feedings.

Milk that drips out into a plastic cup between feedings should not be fed to the baby. Since it's being kept next to the woman's warm body, the warm milk is a perfect breeding ground for bacteria.

After women resume making love, it is common for them to leak during orgasm, although some women do not.

You can avoid plugged ducts and breast infections. If you notice a small pea-shaped lump in your breast while nursing, it is probably a plugged duct. A plugged duct seems to be a small accumulation of milk or dead cells in a duct (the passageway that the milk travels through). It is a common and harmless minor problem for nursing mothers, although many women don't know what to call it. Plugged ducts usually go away in a day or two of frequent nursings. If you notice a lumpy area on one side, try starting all feedings on that side. The baby's nursing will move the plug down the duct and out.*

Did you notice that the advice for plugged ducts is the same as the advice on avoiding painful nipples and engorgement? *Use*

---

*Of course, a lump that does not move at all after frequent nursing should be checked by a practitioner who is familiar with nursing breasts.

short frequent nursings to keep the milk flowing. Internal breast problems usually happen when the milk does not flow. A woman who suddenly stops nursing completely is quite likely to get a breast infection. When you decide you want to wean (stop nursing), be sure to do so gradually.

Plugged ducts can also be caused by external pressure such as wearing a nursing bra that is too tight. Remove the bra or use a bra extender.

Although sore nipples and other breast problems are fairly common among women who aren't taught how to avoid them, they don't usually make women quit nursing.

Why do so many women give up nursing and switch to formula feeding? There's only one common reason: *women give up nursing because they think they don't have enough milk.* Often, the women do have plenty of milk but they lack confidence. Someone says to her, "That baby's crying—how do we know you have enough milk?" and right away, the new mother starts to have doubts.

How to tell if the baby's getting enough milk? You can't tell by giving him a bottle. Babies have such strong sucking needs they will take a bottle (or pacifier or thumb). So that's no test.

You can tell if your baby is getting enough if:

• he has six or more wet diapers a day, and you are not giving him extra water
• he is gaining a pound a month or more
• you are nursing eight to ten times in twenty-four hours

Sometimes women really don't have enough milk. Why? The usual reason why women don't have enough milk is that they're not nursing often enough. Instead of nursing frequently, they nurse every four hours. These women don't understand supply and demand, which means, simply: *The more you nurse, the more milk you will have.*

Bottles and food can make your baby go longer between nursings. But if you nurse less one day, you will make less milk the following day. When your baby seems extra hungry, you can nurse him more often. That way, you will build up your milk supply. Remember, the more you nurse, the more milk you will have.

All babies have growth spurts or days when they are hungrier and need more milk. All babies, breast- or bottle-fed, need more milk as they get bigger. For many babies this happens between the tenth to fourteenth day, again between the fourth and sixth week, next around the third month, and then again around the fifth to sixth month.

When you're breast-feeding, you can't just tell your breasts to produce more ounces. *But if you go along with your baby's need to nurse frequently (which usually lasts about forty-eight hours), your milk supply will be built up.* If you fill up your baby with a bottle or cereal, your supply will not increase. The times when growth spurts are occurring won't be hard on your nerves if you appreciate how well your body can function. You can produce all the milk your baby needs even though he is growing. To do this you should maintain a good diet and drink plenty of liquids.

Don't think you should stall off the baby until your breasts have time to fill up. There is plenty of milk after one and a half to two hours—you just can't see it or feel it. After a week or two your breasts won't seem so full anymore. Remember that this is because the swelling (not the milk) goes away.

When you are at home with the baby, you should expect that he or she will sometimes cry and act fussy—often for no reason that anyone can find. If you just go ahead and nurse your baby—even if it is only for comfort—you will find breast-feeding rather easy.

Mothers who believe that the only purpose of nursing is for hunger withhold the breast when they imagine that the baby shouldn't be hungry. As a group, they find breast-feeding very difficult.

Mothers who try to nurse on a schedule also find breast-feeding difficult. It is hard to deal with a crying baby when the clock says feeding time is an hour away. Nursing is easier than trying to stall him off or listening to him cry. Breast milk is so easy to digest that a new baby may need to nurse after one to three hours in the daytime. Babies go longer between feedings as they get older.

❧ *Your Doctor Appointment*

THE POSTPARTUM CHECKUP

The average hospital stay is two to three days for a vaginal birth and four to six nights for a cesarean section. Most insurance companies only allow for this much postpartum care, so you don't have too much choice about extending your stay (unless, that is, you're willing to pay hospital costs, which can run into hundreds of dollars a day, out of your own pocket).

Your doctor will probably stop in once a day during your hospital stay to check on your recovery progress. Upon your release from the hospital, your doctor will probably give you a list of instructions similar to this:

- Delay dieting
- If receiving other medication attention, or any medication, inform physician that you are breast-feeding.
- No tub baths or swimming
- No tampons or douching
- Refrain from sexual intercourse
- Avoid bending, heavy lifting, driving, and active sports

These strictures will be lifted once you have your postpartum checkup, which is usually within four to six weeks after a vaginal birth. (If you delivered by cesarean, you'll probably see your doctor two weeks after, and then again four to six weeks after delivery.) In the meantime, the following symptoms are warning signs that warrant a call to your doctor:

- Cracked, painful nipples or painful, red, hard breasts
- Fever over 100.4° F (may signal the presence of infection)
- Increase in lochia flow after prolonged ebb
- Burning during urination
- Pain, tenderness, or a hardened area in your calves or thighs (may be a sign of a blood clot)
- Foul-smelling vaginal discharge
- Unusual or increased pain in your episiotomy or cesarean-section site
- Bright-red vaginal bleeding

‫ *Your Diet*

Nursing requires you to follow a balanced diet identical to the one you ate during pregnancy. In fact, the standard prescription—that you need to eat an additional five hundred calories a day during breast-feeding—is probably wrong (and may be why some nursing mothers have had difficulty dropping their pregnancy weight in the past).

The most recent research suggests that a nursing woman's metabolic rate changes to become more efficient at using calories. That means you need fewer calories than previously thought to nourish your baby well and nourish yourself well, while, at the same time, your body slowly burns up its fat stores to lose pregnancy pounds. So it doesn't make sense to consciously force yourself to include more foods while nursing. Instead, try to follow the dictates of your appetite and of your common sense. If your hunger is satisfied, if you're reasonably energetic, and if you are slowly but surely dropping your pregnancy pounds, you can be assured that the volume of food you are eating is adequate and healthy.

Just as the quantity of food in your breast-feeding diet will be more or less the same as it was in your pregnancy diet, the quality will be the same, too. You need to eat lots of fruits and vegetables, get adequate protein, ample complex carbohydrates, etc. Particularly important while nursing is to drink your quart of milk a day, since breast-feeding can drain your bone-calcium stores. Drinking plenty of liquids is important, too, since your body needs fluid to produce milk.

You'll also need to continue to avoid freshwater sport and large open-ocean fish, since the contaminants they might contain can easily be transferred to your milk. Alcohol, except in very moderate, occasional amounts, is not recommended. Preliminary evidence indicates that breast-fed babies whose mothers have at least one drink a day may experience delayed motor abilities. And, of course, smoking and drug-taking should be avoided.

In addition, some foods may make the taste of your milk unpleasant to your baby and/or may give your baby gas. Hot, strongly spiced foods, garlic, broccoli, cabbage, and brussels sprouts are foods that are traditionally mentioned as problem-producing. You'll probably need to do a little of your own sleuthing, since your baby may not react to what you eat at all or may react to unexpected things. For example, the night I ate salmon, my three-week-old daughter experienced a terrible gas attack. The next day, my sister asked me what I had eaten. At the mention of salmon she exclaimed that her newborn daughter had experienced the same reaction. Although many doctors deny that what you eat can, via your milk, give your baby gas, breast-feeding mothers from around the world and throughout the ages have reported seeing a very definite cause and effect.

ॐ Your Workout

EXERCISES FOR THE EARLY POSTPARTUM PERIOD

By six weeks postpartum, you should be able to begin easing back into a strenuous exercise routine (jogging, swimming, aerobic dance, etc.), unless, of course, you had a cesarean, in which case you'll need several weeks longer to recuperate.

If you've had a vaginal delivery, you'll want to begin doing Kegel exercises immediately postpartum (see "Your Workout," p. 136). These will help tone up your stretched vaginal muscles and speed up healing of the vaginal/anal area, too. You can also begin the four exercises below right away (if you've had a cesarean, however, wait several weeks and get your doctor's okay first). These exercises will start to get your abdominal muscles back in shape, and will keep your spine limber and pain-free.

1. *Controlled abdominal breathing:* Inhale deeply, hold the breath for a moment, then exhale slowly at the same time as you pull in your stomach muscles. You can do this walking, standing, or lying down, whenever and as often as you can remember to do it during the course of a day.

2. *Chin to chest:* Lie flat on your back, with no pillow. Lift your head so that your chin touches your chest and, simultaneously, contract your stomach muscles. Do this daily, as often as you can remember to.

3. *Full body stretch:* While lying flat, lift your arms over your head. Reach with your fingers and extend your legs at the heels to pull your body in opposite directions. Repeat as frequently as you can.

4. *Spine stretch:* Lie flat, with your knees bent, feet flat. Gradually lower one leg and, at the same time, push your spine down, into the bed. Repeat with the other leg; do as often as you can find time to do it.

❧ *Your Feelings*

WHAT IS "NORMAL"?

The days and weeks following the birth of your baby are likely to be charged by emotional highs, lows and a myriad of moods in between. My hope is that the reference below provides you with reassurance that what you're feeling is normal and, even, universal.

Sense of relief. Your relief at no longer having to be anxious about labor, at no longer needing to worry about the health of the fetus, and at having survived delivery may be surprisingly profound. You may simply not have realized how anxious you were about everything until it is all over.

Feelings of accomplishment. Especially if you feel you handled the physical stress of labor and delivery well, you may feel strong and confident. But even if you are disappointed with how your labor unfolded, you may still feel very proud of your baby.

A need to "debrief." Don't be surprised if you find you want to recount your birth scenario over and over again, in great detail. Childbirth is an extraordinary event, and talking it over helps you to make sense of it. Also, telling others about important events seems to be one of the ways we integrate these experiences into our personal histories and into a new conception of ourselves.

Feelings of emptiness. This may come as a surprise (at least it did to me), but you may find you feel a sense of loss, a sort of bittersweet sadness, about not having a baby kicking inside you anymore.

A *sense of heightened emotionality*. You may not exactly feel sad or depressed during the first few postpartum days, but instead, more vulnerable, sensitive, and open to emotion. A news item that you might not normally react to may now leave you brimming with tears, for instance. A baby's cry (especially your baby's) may suddenly seem like one of the most poignant things in the universe.

Overwhelmed by the fact that you delivered via cesarean. Having a cesarean can trigger a wide range of feelings that affect your self-esteem. Especially if you had little time to prepare for the fact that you were to have one, you may feel confused, sad, and victimized, as well as angry at having had to experience all that labor pain for "nothing." You may also feel that you've missed something important, some womanly rite of passage, by not having delivered vaginally. You may be disappointed in yourself, too, as if you "should have done better."

Of course, not every woman experiences a cesarean as a "crisis." In fact, some are quite happy and relieved to "have gotten it over with," while others prefer a cesarean birth because they feel it is easier on them and their baby.

If, however, you do feel frustrated and disappointed, the best way to let go of your thoughts of "what might have been" is to rerun all the events that led up to the decision to deliver via cesarean. Ask your doctor to recount all the details of the medical management of the birth. Doing this can help reinforce your confidence that the right thing was done, and that, in the end, most of the events were beyond your control. In other words, you are not "guilty" in any way for the fact that you needed a c-section. *It's not your fault!* Also, it helps not to have unrealistic expectations of yourself. So give yourself time to mourn the loss of your dream of a vaginal birth. The less pressure you put on yourself to "put on a happy face" about it, the more quickly you'll pass through the grieving process.

Worried about bonding. Not everyone falls in love with their baby at first sight; some find it takes weeks or months for full-blown, deep "mother love" to set in and take hold. As long as you don't feel continually hostile toward or detached from your baby (which, if you do, should be a signal to seek professional advice), and do feel a relationship slowly evolving, don't worry, you'll "bond" to your baby and fall in love, with time.

A sense of letdown. Especially if you felt giddy and euphoric the first few postpartum days, you may experience passing episodes of depression or feel psychologically "at sea" at times in the ensuing weeks. These ups and downs in mood are probably partly the result of hormonal shifts your body makes as it adjusts to a nonpregnant state.

Disappointment. If you had a long, difficult labor and/or the birth did not go as you had hoped, you may feel disappointment, regret, and anger. You may also be filled with self-criticism and feelings of being a failure. But though it may take some effort, you should work on forgiving yourself and letting go of these negative feelings. The more you dwell on your disappointment, the greater risk you run of missing out on the specialness of the first weeks of your baby's life. And, later, when you look back, what will be important is not how your baby was born but *your baby* and how he or she looked, felt, and acted as an infant. Above all, keep reminding yourself that all births are unique. Just because your friend X labored, delivered, and recovered with tremendous ease, it doesn't mean you are somehow "weaker" because you've had a harder time.

Concern for the future. In the postpartum months, your baby is likely to be uppermost in your mind. And you may find that, besides trying to decipher the puzzle of what his or her immediate needs are, you fantasize and wonder a great deal about the future and how your baby will cope with growing up.

Lonely. As postpartum life begins settling into a routine and the baby becomes the primary focus of most people's attention, you may long for some "mothering," special attention, and support yourself. Although you probably wish others would just instinctively know you could use a hand, realistically, you'll probably need to ask for it.

Feelings of inadequacy. If you have a baby whose behavior is difficult to decode or who is difficult to comfort, there are likely to be times in these early months when you doubt your competence as a mother. But the older your baby gets, the easier it will be to care for and understand him or her; with that will come feelings of self-confidence.

Anger at your mate. You may feel intensely resentful of your partner if a) you feel overwhelmed by your baby's dependence on you; b) you aren't receiving what you perceive as enough help from him; and/or c) he is your sole link to the outside, "adult" world. In reverse, your partner may feel emotionally off-balance if he was accustomed to a) being the main object of your attention; b) receiving help from you (not giving it); and c) your being independent and self-sufficient. If your relationship is basically good and strong, you'll be able to ride out these rough first weeks as each of you gradually adjusts to your new role and develops new expectations of each other.

Bored. Especially if you worked during your pregnancy, you may be surprised at how much boredom there can be in taking care of the baby full-time.

Passing regrets. When you're exhausted after being up all night with a crying baby, and when you seem to be either breastfeeding or changing a diaper at any given moment, it's not unusual to think, "Why on earth did I have a baby?" Don't feel guilty. It's the rare mother who doesn't have this thought.

Profound happiness. Nurturing a baby and watching him or her grow and thrive can add a whole new dimension of happiness to your life. Although I experienced some weepy spells, boredom, and all the rest, I found my daughter mostly brought pleasure into my day-to-day existence. In fact, I never expected caring for a baby would be punctuated with as much sheer joy as it did, nor did I realize how fulfilled, self-assured, and "grounded" her birth would make me feel.

❧   *FEELING DOWN?*   ❧

If you are feeling down, you may be suffering from one of these syndromes:

Postpartum Blues: The "blues" are very common; they may be caused by the dramatic hormonal shifts you experience postpartum. The "blues" are characterized by transient irritability, sadness, crying spells, and mood swings, which can last anywhere from a few days to a few weeks. The best remedy for the "blues" is to simply get out of the house—even if it's only for a short walk. It helps to keep your energy up, too, by eating right.

Postpartum Depression (PPD): This is a more serious, less common syndrome characterized by changes in appetite, an inability to concentrate, loss of self-esteem, insomnia, and prolonged feelings of helplessness and anxiety. PPD can last up to a year and can hamper your ability to properly care for your baby. Ask your obstetrician about seeking professional help and/or contact Depression After Delivery, P.O. Box 1282, Morrisville, PA 19067, 215-295-3994.

Postpartum Psychosis: This is an extremely rare disorder (affecting about one out of every one thousand new mothers according to some estimates), which probably only afflicts women who were, prepregnancy, predisposed to mental illness. The disorder is characterized by delusion, hallucinations, and a loss of one's sense of reality. Women suffering from postpartum psychosis are at risk for harming their babies and so should receive immediate psychiatric treatment.

‰ *Your Lifestyle*

THE NEW ADDITION TO THE FAMILY

A baby changes everything, and I mean *everything* in your life. All the little things you were able to do without thinking, whenever you felt like it, such as taking a shower, sitting down for dinner, deciding to telephone a friend, are likely to get interrupted, put off, or require lots of preplanning once you have a baby. At first, I found this new fact of my life difficult to handle. I kept waiting for things to get "back to normal." It was only after I finally accepted that things would probably never "get back to normal" that my mood and outlook began to improve. Once I stopped expecting to have an uninterrupted, spontaneous lifestyle, once I made peace with the reality that my movements could no longer be self-centered, it all disturbed me much less. Not only did everything become a lot easier, but I was even able to laugh about it when my daughter would yet again, with her uncanny timing, shriek for attention just as I was sitting down to eat.

If you only focus on the things you can't do or can't have now that you have a baby, you're likely to be dissatisfied, angry, and filled with a sense of loss most of the time. It is far better to reinvent yourself and to shift your expectations. That way you'll be able to enjoy your newcomer and appreciate the way he or she enriches, enhances, and brings a profound new dimension of nurturance and love into your life.

ಶಿ   *WHEN A NEWBORN DIES*   ಶಿ

Most couples find that the loss of a child to miscarriage, still-birth, or infant death is no less painful or grief-filled than it would be if a long-known and loved family member died. In fact, grieving a newborn's loss may even be harder, since a couple's sadness is very often complicated by feelings of inadequacy, shame, and powerlessness. What's more, parents, grandparents, or friends can sometimes make things more difficult by underestimating the emotional impact of the death and by expecting a couple to "get over it" quickly.

Luckily, however, more and more health professionals today are aware of the depth of feelings a couple may experience upon loss of a newborn. For example, unlike before, when a deceased baby was quickly taken away after birth, most doctors and nurses now encourage parents to hold, see, and name the baby. That's because almost all mental health experts find that not only is what a parent conjures in his or her imagination far worse than what the parent will see (even if the baby has died due to a serious birth defect), but holding the lost baby helps the parents properly face the loss and go on to recover from it.

The support groups listed below can go a long way toward helping parents cope with the intense grief and other emotional reverberations that a newborn's death provokes. For a series of sensitive, thoughtful pamphlets on newborn death, you can also contact the Centering Corporation, Box 3367, Omaha, NE 68103-0367, 402-553-1200.

Resolve through Sharing, La Crosse Lutheran Hospital, 1910 South Avenue, La Crosse, WI 54601; 608-785-0530, ext. 3696.

Aiding a Mother Experiencing Neonatal Death (AMEND), 4324 Berrywick Terrace, St. Louis, MO 63128; 314-487-7582.

A Source of Help in Airing and Resolving Experiences (SHARE), St. Elizabeth Hospital, 220 West Lincoln Street, Belleville, IL 62220; 618-234-2415.

AFTERWORD

In many ways, the way I've responded to motherhood (so far, at least—my daughter, Adelaide, is one and a half years old as I write this) has been similar to the way I responded to pregnancy. I've not been an overly worried nervous wreck, but then again, I'm not a completely laid-back "natural," either. Especially in the first months, I sought late-night advice (thank God for my sister!), searched for solutions in childcare books, worried about "quality time," and wondered, on any given day, if Adelaide was eating/sleeping/eliminating/drinking/growing enough or too much.

One thing I have found truly inspiring are these words from Grantly Dick-Read in *Childbirth without Fear:*

> Every infant is a law unto itself which should be studied by the mother.

I remember this simple sentence whenever I'm tempted to compare Adelaide's growth, behavior, or development to that of other children. It also helps bolster my confidence in myself; it reminds me that I should trust my instincts (since I really do know my baby better than anyone else) and stick to my guns, even if what I feel is right is contrary to what others advise. (Be forewarned: new mothers are barraged with advice!!)

Growing into my role as "Mom" has been an adventure, with lots of surprises. I never could have predicted, pre-Adelaide, how deeply I would fall in love with her, how moving I would find a simple affectionate pat, how absorbing I would find her first efforts to turn herself over. Of course, there have been "down" times too, moments when I've felt hemmed in by my responsibility to her and moments when I've felt truly inadequate (there were times when Addie, as a newborn, simply couldn't be comforted, and her cries pierced my heart and made me feel inept and useless). But the cliché, "This too shall pass," really holds true with babies—just when you're at your patience's end, your baby is likely to transform and enter some new phase or stage. In fact, since Addie's birth, I've learned to have much more faith in the power, process, and prospect of change and development.

I wish you the best of times with your baby. And I hope that this book has not only helped you through this pregnancy, but will be useful if and when you have another child. In fact, I'd love to hear from you: your feedback, questions, and criticisms can help make any revised editions even better. You can write me, Janis Graham, author of *Your Pregnancy Companion*, c/o Pocket Books, 1230 Avenue of the Americas, New York, NY 10020.

INDEX